Charles Gavan Duffy

A Bird's-Eye View of Irish History

Charles Gavan Duffy

A Bird's-Eye View of Irish History

ISBN/EAN: 9783744734042

Printed in Europe, USA, Canada, Australia, Japan

Cover: Foto ©ninafisch / pixelio.de

More available books at **www.hansebooks.com**

IRISH PEOPLE'S EDITION.

A Bird's-Eye View

OF

IRISH HISTORY.

BY

SIR CHARLES GAVAN DUFFY,
K.C.M.G.

DUBLIN:
JAMES DUFFY AND CO., Limited,
15 WELLINGTON QUAY.

DUBLIN:
Printed by Edmund Burke and Co.,
61 & 62 Gt. Strand Street.

TO
THE RIGHT REV. JAMES DONNELLY,

Bishop of Clogher,

ETC., ETC.,

MONAGHAN.

I DESIRE, my dear Lord, to associate this little book with your honoured name, because its appearance in its present shape is largely owing to suggestions which you were good enough to make to me on the subject; and, still more, because your fruitful life and labours are devoted to the well-remembered places where I first studied Irish History, and gathered the traditions and memories which interpret the past better than the historian.

C. G. D.

Nice, May, 1882.

PREFACE TO "THE IRISH PEOPLE'S EDITION."

THE publishers, whose property it is, propose to issue this little volume at a price which will make it universally accessible. The first edition found a welcome among English and foreign thinkers; and, perhaps, helped in some degree to place transactions in a right point of view, which were misunderstood because they had been persistently misrepresented. But its main purpose was to be useful at home. We do not know our own story, except vaguely and inexactly; but the history of the Past is the master-key to whatever problems are perplexing in the transactions of our own day.

I have resisted the temptation to make additions to this little book, in order that it may remain what it was designed to be—an Essay that may be read in a single evening, and where those who cannot study the sources of Irish History for themselves may easily find whatever inquiry and controversy have established respecting its cardinal epochs.

VILLA CORNELIA, NICE,
26th Feb., 1884.

PREFACE.

THE separate publication of the "Bird's-Eye View" of Irish History has been so often recommended by critics, that I have determined to comply with the suggestion. A Paris publisher, indeed, anticipated the design by detaching it from "Young Ireland," for reproduction in an influential review, *Le Monde Catholique*, and afterwards in a separate brochure for French readers.*

When it was first written my chief difficulty was to compress the necessary facts into such a space that the narrative might not destroy the symmetry of the book into which it was introduced as an historical background. The present form admits of fuller treatment, and I have considerably enlarged the plan. But it is still no more than a hasty glance at a subject which will repay careful

---

* Histoire d'Irlande à Vol d'Oiseau. Traduit d'Anglais par Marie Wilson Cowley.—Paris: Bleriot et Gautier, 1882.

and conscientious study. The story is not carried beyond 1840. The history of the ten memorable years which followed, are written in detail in the work from which this chapter has been borrowed.

It is not convenient to overlay so small a manual by a list of authorities. But I have stated nothing which I have not ascertained to rest on solid grounds, and the subject has been a study with me from boyhood.

I have been careful to keep this little book within such limits that it may be conveniently read in a single evening, but to make it full enough to furnish at least a tolerably complete flying survey of our history. It would best answer its purpose if it encouraged young men to inquire for themselves, and served them as a primer and skeleton map for such studies. Perhaps it would be of use also to strangers anxious for some light on the question which they find so perplexing, why Ireland, with all her natural resources and native vigour is so perpetually poor and discontented ?

Nice, May, 1882.

A BIRD'S-EYE VIEW

OF

IRISH HISTORY.

MANY men refrain from reading Irish history as sensitive and selfish persons refrain from witnessing human suffering. But it is a branch of knowledge as indispensable to the statesman or publicist as morbid anatomy to the surgeon. To prescribe remedies without ascertaining the seat of the disease, and the habits of the patient, is empiricism and quackery. For Irishmen there is no portion of the annals of mankind so profitable a study. It will teach them to understand themselves and their country; a knowledge essential to national prosperity, but which is far from being common amongst us. It will teach them how much we have often to unlearn; for writers of great authority have ignorantly or wilfully caricatured our history, till there is scarcely a transaction concerning which it is more necessary to inquire what are the facts which may be accepted and relied upon, than what is the skilful and current misrepresentation of them which ought to be rejected.

In the rapid survey I propose to make I will omit whatever can be omitted without direct loss, and touch only on events the consequences of which were still traceable in the habits and character of the people in the middle of the nineteenth century.

The history of England, inextricably connected with ours from an early period, I assume to be familiar to the reader. He must know both stories to solve the cardinal problem of their long connection; why the larger island gradually attained a prosperity nearly unexampled in the world, and a settled government under which public and individual liberty are as secure as they ever were in any community; while the smaller island, lying under the same sky, and, professedly, subject to the same system of government, is poorer and more disorderly and discontented than any nation in Europe?

The aboriginal inhabitants of Ierné, like the Ancient Britons across the neighbouring channel, or the Gauls on the nearest mainland, were conquered at an early period by a people who identified themselves so completely with their new possessions, that they have come to be regarded as the type of the native race. It was several centuries.

before Christ* that an expedition of Celts from Spain, led by a chief whose name in its Latinised form is Milesius, landed on the island, and after some fierce fighting obtained complete possession of it. They were the Normans of that era, these Milesians, better armed and trained than the natives; disciplined in a higher civilization, and politic enough to desire not to destroy but to absorb the conquered people. After the conquest the country (according to Celtic traditions) was divided between Heber and Heremon, sons of Milesius, to one or other of whom all the native families of ancient blood delight to trace their pedigree; and to this day the favourite name for an Irishman in poetry and romance is a Milesian. Munster and Leinster were assigned to Heber, Ulster and Connaught to Heremon; and in after times, when the island came to have an Ard-Reigh or chief king, a cause of constant war was the question, whether he should be chosen from the country of Heber or the country of Heremon?

There were protracted and merciless feuds among the Milesian chiefs and their successors for many generations, feuds such as, nearly two thousand years later, desolated England in the Wars of the Roses. But the annals of every people with patriarchal customs and institutions,

---

*The precise date is much disputed, and historians have fixed it at eras as widely apart as the fourteenth, and the second, centuries before the Incarnation.

begin in the same way. They feel unlimited devotion to the sept or tribe, and only a wavering loyalty to the union of tribes constituting the realm ; they ravage and massacre in the name of a chief who has suffered some indignity from a rival, and answer coldly to the call of a king who is enforcing a national right, or resisting an invader.

They were a long-rooted dynasty, these Milesian kings. The Irish annalists affirm that the island was ruled in succession by more than a hundred and fifty native princes before the conversion to Christianity. The most noted of the Pagan kings was Odlam Fodla, who established the Celtic equivalent for a parliament, a triennial conference (called in the native tongue a *Fes*) of Princes, Chiefs, Brehons, and Bards at Tara, where a stately palace was erected for their reception, built, doubtless, like the early temples and palaces of Greece, of timber from their abundant forests.* This king is described as a founder of colleges and a patron of learned men—a character peculiarly honoured in Irish annals. Another Pagan King attained the formidable title of Conn of the Hundred Battles. His grand-

---

* The Brehons were the judges, the Bards and Seanachies the annalists of the kingdom. They were largely endowed with land and cattle, and protected in their peaceful pursuits from the violence of the times. The offices were hereditary in certain families ; and the favoured class were trained from youth upwards in the knowledge and traditions of their profession.

son Cormac-O'Conn* was contemporary with Ossian, the Homer of the Celts, and Finn MacComal (called Fingal by the Scotch), who is still a familiar name in Ireland for his immense strength and subtlety, and as leader of the Fenian Militia.† The last of the Pagan Kings was Dathy, who was killed by lightning at the foot of the Alps, where, like some of his predecessors, he had led a predatory expedition, in search not of territory but of plunder.

From the earliest glimpse we catch of them in history, the Celts of Ireland were what they still continue. A robust and warlike race, vehement in their passions, generous in their friendships, hospitable, pious, tenacious of old habits, and possessed with an extraordinary reverence for whatever authority they recognise as legitimate. But, on the other hand, lightly moved to anger, too easily elated

---

* O is equivalent to grandson. Mac to son.

† The nearest coast of Britain is little over seven leagues distant from the peninsula lying between Strangford Lough and the Irish Sea, and there was constant intercourse between the neighbouring islands. A horde of adventurous Celts from Ireland settled in the present Argyleshire, and they and their descendants, and new recruits from time to time, became so numerous that North Britain was called Scotia Minor, or Little Ireland; Ireland at that era being known in poetry as Scotia, probably from the Scotic or Scythic ancestry of the people. These adventurers carried with them the poems and traditions of their country, and in modern times Ossian and his heroes have been claimed as Scots He was a Scot to the same extent that Shakespeare was an American colonist.

or depressed, and governed by an intense individuality which makes it hard to subordinate personal claims to those of a competitor, or to forgive an indignity. The native dress as it is first seen, and as it continued till the time of the Tudors, consisted of parti-coloured vest and trews (which still survives in the Highland plaid), mantle, barret (or cap, resembling the Phrygian cap which the French have named the cap of liberty), and shirts dyed saffron colour, and in the case of princes and chiefs, of prodigious amplitude.

Many of the early kings met a violent death, and ungenerous critics find in the fact a ground to charge the Irish race with inherent turbulence. But cotemporary kings of all the nations not held down by the sword of Rome, met a similar fate; and at a much later period Roman emperors themselves, raised to the purple which symbolised supremacy over the whole human race, had as short and uncertain a tenure of power, and as tragic an end, as befel the Pagan kings of Ierné.*

The Irish race first felt the contagion of a common

---

* The name Ierné, the first given to the island, signifies in the Phœnician language, "the uttermost point;" the most western promontory of Spain was so called before the discovery of Ireland, when the title was probably transferred to correspond with the new fact. No land more westerly was known before the discoveries of Columbus Erin was the name used by the natives.

purpose not in war, but in labours of devotion and charity. Lying on the extreme verge of Europe, the last land then known to the adventurous Scandinavian, and beyond which fable had scarcely projected its dreams, it was in the fifth century since the Redemption that Christianity reached them. Patricius, a Celt of Gaul it is said, carried into Erin as a slave by one of the Pagan kings, some of whom made military expeditions to North and South Britain, and even to the Alps and the Loire, became the Apostle of Ireland.* Patrick escaped from slavery, was educated at Rome, but in mature manhood insisted on returning to the place of his bondage, to preach Christianity to a people who seem to have exercised over the imagination of the Apostle the same spell of sympathy which in later times subdued strangers of many nations. He was received with extraordinary favour, and before his death nearly the whole island had embraced Christianity.

The coming of Patrick took place in the year of our Lord 432, and he laboured for sixty years after; planting churches and schools, rooting out the practices and monuments of Paganism, and disciplining the people in religion and humanity. It was a noble service, and it impressed itself for ever on the memory of the race whom he served.

---

* The king who made Patrick a slave is known in our annals as Nial of the Nine Hostages, and was the ancestor of the O'Neills.

Between forty and fifty generations of men have since been born in the island, and have spread over the earth as missionaries, scholars, soldiers, artisans and labourers, and no generation, at home or in exile, in prosperity or poverty, has failed on his fête day, which has become the national festival of Ireland, to commemorate the name of the Apostle who brought the knowledge of God to the Irish race.

In the succeeding century the Church which he planted became possessed by a passion which it has never entirely lost, the passion for missionary enterprise. Its Fathers projected the conversion of the fierce natives of the Continent to the new creed of humility and self-denial, and by the same humane agents which Patrick had employed in Ireland—persuasion and prayer; a task as generous as any of which history has preserved the record. In this epoch Ireland may, without exaggeration, be said to have been a Christian Greece, the nurse of science and civilisation. The Pagan annals of the country are overlaid by fable and extravagance, but the foundation of Oxford or the mission of St. Augustine does not lie more visibly within the boundaries of legitimate history than the Irish schools, which attracted students from Britain and Gaul, and sent out missionaries through the countries now known as Western Europe. Among the forests of Germany, on the desert shores of the Hebrides, in the camp of Alfred, at the court of Charlemagne, in the capital of the Christian world, where Michelet describes their eloquence as charming the counsellors of the Emperor, there might be found the fervid preachers and subtle doctors of the Western Isle. It was then that the island won the title still fondly cherished, "*insula sanctorum.*" The Venerable Bede describes nobles and students at this epoch as quitting the island of Britain to seek education in Ireland, and he tells us that the hospitable Celts found them teachers, books, food and shelter at the cost of the nation. The school at Armagh, where St. Patrick had established the primacy of the Church, is reputed to have attracted seven thousand students, and there were schools at Lismore, Bangor, Clonmacnoise, and Mayo which rivalled it in importance. Monasteries multiplied in a still greater number, and with results as beneficial. "The Monks," says a learned critic,* "fixed their habitations in deserts which they cultivated with their own hands, and rendered the most delightful spots in the kingdom. These deserts in time became well governed cities."

Writers who are little disposed to make any other concession to Ireland admit that this was a period of extraordinary intellectual activity, and of memorable services to civilization. The arts, as far as they were the handmaidens of religion, attained a surprising

---

* Mr. O'Connor, the Librarian of Stowe.

development. The illuminated copies of the Scripture, the croziers and chalices which have come down to us from those days, the Celtic crosses and Celtic harps, the bells and tabernacles, are witnesses of a distinct and remarkable national culture. The people were still partly shepherds and husbandmen, partly soldiers, ruled by the Chief, the Brehon, and the Priest. Modern philosophers who deplore their fate would find it hard to discover any period, before or since, when they were so prosperous and happy.*

After this generous work had obtained a remarkable success, it was disturbed by contests with the Sea Kings. The Northmen who had established themselves in Britain and Gaul, and before whom even the Capital of the world in those days could not make effectual resistance, were equally successful in Ireland. They found a country rich in corn-lands, cattle, and "fishful rivers," and containing immense depositories of gold and precious stones in its churches and colleges, and they came in successive swarms to enjoy the plunder. Some of the expeditions consisted of more than a hundred ships, filled with trained warriors, who speedily fortified for themselves the strongest positions on the coasts, and laid the foundation of maritime towns. The Cathedral and city of St. Patrick, the schools

---

*Those who require specific evidence of the learning and missionary labours of the early Irish will find the testimony of French and English writers on the subject in the Appendix.

of Bangor, the cloisters of Clonmacnoise, and many more
seats of piety and learning, fell into their hands. The
sacred vessels of the altar were turned into drinking cups,
and the missals, blazing with precious stones, were torn
from their costly bindings to furnish ornaments for their
sword hilts, and gifts to the Scalds who sang their achievements. These pagans burned monasteries, sacked churches,
and murdered women and priests, for plunder or sport.
Their creed was framed, like that of the Saracens
who threatened the existence of Christendom four
centuries later, to enlist the strongest human passions in
its service. It taught that it was their right to take without stint or scruple whatever they could win by the sword,
and that if they fell in battle they would be transported to
a delicious country, where they would renew their warlike
sports, and be recreated after toil at majestic feasts in the
Hall of Oden, and with the blandishments of celestial
nymphs. The native princes had frequent successes
against the invaders, took many of their strong places, and
compelled them to make submission from time to time, but
fresh expeditions eager for plunder still arrived from Scan-
dinavia, and renewed the struggle, which continued generation after generation.*

---

* One of the most formidable of the invaders, a chief named Turgesius,
is said to have subjected the invaded race to the last humiliation in
requiring them to yield up the daughter of a native Christian prince to
be one of his many wives. But this prince, as the tradition runs,

Before the dangers and troubles of a long internecine war, the School of the West gradually dwindled away, and it had fallen into complete decay before Brian Borhoime, at the beginning of the eleventh century, finally subdued the invaders. Brian, who had been a soldier from his youth, only came to the throne as Ardreigh in his seventieth year. The younger brother of a provincial prince (whom he served loyally, and succeeded at his death), he had risen slowly, by valour and policy, to the foremost place. Though he was eminently endowed by nature, and prepared by discipline and experience, to exercise authority, it must not be concealed that he snatched the supreme office from a man scarcely less fit or worthy to possess it. King Malachy had won many victories over the Danes, had distinguished himself by restoring schools of learning which they had destroyed, and re-establishing the royal authority sorely shaken by their success. The annalists describe the tranquillity of his epoch as a sort of Golden Age. He recalled to their homes, they aver, two thousand prisoners, hostages, and refugees, and made peace and security prevail universally in the land.* He gave, at any

---

affecting to consent to the shameful proposal, sent a troop of beardless youths disguised as maidens, who, in the midst of the marriage feast, slaughtered the Danish chiefs, and delivered a wide region from their power. The story is probably as mythical as the legends with which the early history of Rome, and of all ancient nations, is adorned.

* " Let all the Irish who are suffering servitude in the land of the

rate, evidence of noble qualities by loyally aiding the new Ardreigh against the foreign enemy. In the year 1014 the Danes summoned allies from the cradle of their race, and from every country where the Sea Kings had founded a settlement, to help them to re-establish their authority in the Western Isle. The battle of Clontarf was fought on Good Friday, in that year, between ten thousand of the invaders, and as many of the natives under Brian, then in his eightieth year. It ended in the complete defeat of the Danes; but the victory was almost counterbalanced by the death of the great king, with his son and grandson. Three generations perished together, and the supreme office reverted to the loyal and generous Malachy, who had done effectual service in the battle. But all the fame of the victory wreathes itself around the memory of the venerable prince who is chronicled in the contemporary "Book of Armagh" as the Emperor (*Imperator*) of the Irish. Brian the Brave holds the same place in the memory of his nation that Alfred the Great won in England by identical services; and to this day wherever enterprise and

---

stranger, return home to their respective houses and enjoy themselves in gladness and in peace."—*Proclamation of King Malachy.*

A few years later annalists place the marvellous incident commemorated in Moore's song, "Rich and rare were the gems she wore," (and which properly belongs to the region of poetry), of a lady, richly arrayed, and carrying a wand adorned with a jewel, who traversed the island in unmolested security.

industry seek new homes,—among the villages of the Mississippi, in the farms and marts of New Zealand, or the cities and gold fields of Australia, you may recognize a settlement of Irish by the rude effigy of a royal warrior, carrying in one hand a cross, and in the other the sword which scattered the northern pirates.*

But other disturbers succeeded to the Danes. In the twelfth century the Norman soldiers, who had conquered England, cast longing eyes on the neighbouring island, and found a footing through the clan and dynastic jealousies to which a pastoral people are peculiarly liable. They came, a recent historian declares, with unconscious irony, to complete the work of civilization happily begun by the Danes.† The population of the island at that time did not reach half a million, and was distributed into a prodigious number of septs. The constitution was little altered from Pagan times. There were still five kings, one of whom was elected Ardreigh, and received tribute from the sub-kings and chiefs, and from such Danish towns as submitted to his authority. The tribute consisted chiefly of cattle, but sometimes of steeds, coats of mail, mantles of state, drinking cups, and wine. In Brian's time it is

---

* Brian left several sons, but none of them was entitled to compete with Malachy for the office of Ardreigh. Those sons were the ancestors of the O'Briens.

† Mr. Froude.

recorded that the Danes of Limerick paid him a pipe of wine for every day in the year. In the Pagan era bondsmen and bondswomen were commonly offered as tribute, and at the period of the invasion slavery had not yet died out. Kings and chiefs were selected on a system which rejected primogeniture. The Celts united with the principle of legitimacy the principle of election, and not the eldest but the most gifted member of the family was chosen. To avoid the dangers of a disputed succession the Roydamna (or successor of the king), was elected during the lifetime of the reigning monarch, and the Tanist during the lifetime of the chief. But the device was not always successful; the question was often remitted to the battle-field. The native poets describe the proud impetuous Celts breaking like a surge against the panoplied ranks of the Norman: "Unequal they engage in battle, the Foreigners and the Gael of Tara! Fine linen shirts on the race of Conn; and the strangers one mass of iron." The native soldiers were armed with spears resembling the modern pike, in the use of which they were very skilful, battle axes, and for close quarters, daggers. But they wore no defensive armour except shields, and sometimes helmets; their heads were generally protected only by a huge mass of hair arranged in flowing locks, known as a *culon*. They were distributed into heavy infantry, called galloglass, and light infantry called kernes, and horsemen

consisting mainly of the chief's nearest kinsmen. The
princes and leaders sometimes wore coats of mail, but,
in general they scorned such a device as unworthy of brave
men. Dublin was merely a Danish settlement at this
era, the seats of authority were the palaces of Tara in
Meath, Emania in Ulster, Cruchan in Connaught, Leighlin
in Leinster, and Cashel in Munster. The natives preferred
to live in the open country; towns, when taken from the
Danes, were commonly abandoned or destroyed.

The Ardreigh at this time was Roderic O'Connor, a just,
patient, laborious man, but wanting the vigorous will and
clear insight which a perilous crisis demands in a leader.
The king of Leinster, Dermid MacMurrough, provoked his
justice by public offences, commencing with the abduction
of the wife of a neighbouring chief, and running through
the whole gamut of crime; and after long patience and
parley he deposed him from his office. MacMurrough fled
to Normandy, where the English king Henry II. was
engaged at the time on the business of his French possessions, and besought his assistance. Henry had long meditated a descent upon Ireland. Some years earlier he had
procured a letter from the Pope, then the referee in all
national quarrels, authorising him to subdue the island,
and reform the Irish Church, which English agents at
Rome described as fallen into dangerous indiscipline.
Henry gave MacMurrough a letter of credence authorizing

him to engage such of his Anglo-Norman knights as might be willing to undertake the enterprise, to accompany him to Ireland. Dermid found in Wales a number of knights then out of employment, and probably out of favour with the king; a curious family group closely connected by blood or marriage, and many of them descended from a common ancestress who, in her youth, had been a paramour of King Henry. The most important recruit was Richard, Earl of Pembroke, also a kinsman of the king; a man best known to posterity by the by-name of Strongbow, conferred on him for his prodigious strength. Dermid, who was still popular with his chiefs, got assistance from them to re-possess himself of his hereditary territory, and several successive expeditions of Normans were allowed to establish themselves in the country; for the settlement of a few mercenary soldiers from Wales seemed a small matter to a people accustomed to the incursions of the Danes. These Norman knights had great advantages not only in arms and discipline, but in the skill of their auxiliaries; their archers were equipped with the cross bow, which could kill at a hundred yards, and had been the chief agent in the overthrow of the Saxons at the battle which delivered England to William the Conqueror. Though their landing was scarcely opposed, Dermid's success was long in doubt. Roderick assembled a great army and drove the invaders and their native allies to shelter and fortify themselves in Dermid's territory, and finally compelled him to make submission, and undertake to dismiss the foreigners, and never to introduce any more. But he was wholly faithless, and he renewed the war as soon as fresh allies arrived from Wales. Dermid, who had passed his sixtieth year before the invasion, was a man of stern mien, and gigantic stature, a courageous soldier, profuse and bountiful in his habits, and not without skill in diplomacy; but boisterous, riotous, and a breaker of promises. He reaped small profit from his alliance with the Normans. The native annalists love to record that within a year of his treason he died of a loathsome disease, abandoned by God and man. But before this event Strongbow had married his daughter Eva, to establish in himself a colourable claim to Dermid's kingdom. He took possession of Dublin, the chief town of Leinster, made it the seat of English authority, and distributed huge cantreds of the tribal land between himself and his attendant knights.

As soon as the first adventurers had established a footing, their liege lord Henry II. King of England claimed the suzerainty, to which he was entitled by feudal law, and came to Ireland accompanied by an army, which for the period was numerous and powerful, to exercise it in person. Henry's claim was to be Lord Paramount; a title carrying only a vague and shadowy authority, which left the native princes in possession of supreme power in their own territories; but with this title he and his successors for more than three centuries contented themselves. His claim was founded on the Pope's grant. Adrian IV. who sat in the chair of Peter at that time was an Englishman, and apparently considered his nation peculiarly fitted to be reformers of morals and conduct. He authorized Henry to inquire into the condition of the Church and the people. "I hold it good and acceptable that, for " extending the borders of the Church, restraining the " progress of vice, for the correction of manners, the " planting of virtue, and the encrease of religion, you " enter this island, and execute therein whatever shall per- " tain to the honour of God and welfare of the land; and " that the people of this land receive you honourably " and reverence you as their lord." It was necessary to satisfy him that the alleged abuses existed, else there was no need of a censor; and in the train of the invaders came the first of a class of functionaries who have reappeared in every subsequent epoch of our history, the official libellers. Gerald Barry, a Welsh monk, known after the custom of the age as *Giraldus Cambrensis*,* wrote an elaborate Latin treatise designed to prejudice the Irish race with the

---

* Giraldus Cambrensis was one of the family party, being a descendant of the same courtesan who was ancestress of so many of the invaders.

Holy See, and justify their subjugation. He did his work so effectually, that Pope Adrian's successor, Alexander III., confirmed the grant of Ireland to the English king, on condition that "the barbarous people" should be "recovered from their filthy life and abominable conversation," and "the rude and disordered Church" reformed; and after seven centuries his libels are still occasionally cited for a kindred purpose, by persons of the same pursuit.

Henry held a synod at Cashel which was attended by the Bishops of Leinster and Munster, who accepted him on the strength of the Pope's letter, and undertook to make any needed reforms in conformity with it. In the same year the bishops who held aloof from the foreigner were summoned to a synod at Tuam by Cathal O'Duffy,* the Archbishop of that province, and applied themselves, as it appears, to ecclesiastical questions, without taking any heed of Henry's pretensions.

The authority established by Henry was acknowledged in Dublin where he fixed the seat of his government, and in a limited territory beyond it known as the Pale; which as the name implies was a rudely fortified camp on a huge scale, whose boundaries shifted with circumstances. Beyond the Pale nothing was changed; the native prince ruled his principality and the native chief ruled his clan as

---

* Cathal, Latinised Catholicus, Anglicised Charles.

of old. Many of them made submission to Henry as bearer of the Pope's letter, and acknowledged him as Lord of Ireland; for such submission was little regarded in an age of constant warfare, if it did not involve the payment of heavy tribute or the concession of territory; and in this case it was specifically provided that they should enjoy all the rights belonging to their office as completely as before the coming of the king. Some of them, however, especially the princes of Ulster, would have no dealings with him on any terms.*

The circumstances of the Invasion are supposed by ill-informed persons to be peculiarly discreditable to Ireland, because one of her native princes brought in the strangers who were aided by other chiefs of the invaded country. It is discreditable, doutless, but it is in no respect peculiar. It was in the same manner the Romans were brought into Gaul, and the Saxons into Britain; and while the Normans under William were mustering their host on the shores of France for the conquest of England, the last Saxon King, before encountering these Frenchmen, had to fight a battle with another Saxon prince, his own brother, at the head of an invasion of Danes.

---

* "He (Henry II.) departed out of Ireland without striking one blow or building one castle, or planting one garrison among the Irish; neither left he behind him one true subject more than those that he found there at his first coming over, which were only the English adventurers."—*Sir John Davies.* (Attorney-General of James I. in Ireland.)

Strongbow was confirmed in immense possessions by the king, but the native annalists record, with natural satisfaction, that in a few years he died of a frightful cancer, having first murdered his son in a gust of brutal anger. Roderick after seventeen years' struggle against fate laid down his crown, and retired into a monastery. The last years of his reign were disturbed by the unnatural rebellion and ingratitude of his children—another cause of reproach to his country, by critics who forget that his contemporary and competitor, Henry II., died in an agony of grief because one of his sons, in alliance with the French King, drove him out of his continental possessions, and another son, who was the dearest object of his affection, secretly abetted the treason.

The transaction in this epoch which Irish students recall with most pleasure is the career of the patriot Archbishop of Dublin, Lorcan, or Laurence, O'Toole. He was a younger son of the O'Byrne of Wicklow, his sister was the wife of Dermid MacMurrough, and mother of Eva who brought Strongbow such a splendid dowry. His birth and office gave him facilities for approaching both parties, which he invariably used to promote the interests not of his kindred, but of his country. He was the counsellor of Roderick in a closer sense than Dunstan was the counsellor of Eadgar, or Lanfranc of William the Conqueror. After memorable labours to unite the native princes in a league

against the invaders, he undertook a mission to the Pope
in concert with Cathal O'Duffy of Tuam to represent the
wrongs to which his nation was subjected, and performed
the duty so effectually that Henry forbade him to return
to Ireland. He died in Normandy, his last recorded words
being a touching lament for his country.* In good time he
was canonized as St. Laurence, and will live for ever in the
memory of his countrymen as the Patriot Archbishop.

Throughout the Middle Ages the Pale was often pushed
into new territories, when a Lord Deputy of unusual
vigour took the field; it sometimes dwindled away when
affairs were going ill in England. It was held at the cost
of frequent wars and constant vigilance, and yielded little
by way of tribute. In every generation an attempt was
made to throw off the foreign yoke. But it was generally
made by an individual chief or a union of chiefs, who
resented some recent wrong; it was imperfectly supported
by the nation, and the troops of the English Lord Deputy
had always Irish allies, who hated an ambitious neighbour
worse than they hated the stranger. It is a marvel to
some critics that the whole population of the island did

---

* "Ah, foolish and insensible people!" he exclaimed in his latest hours, "what will become of you? Who will relieve your miseries? Who will heal you?" When recommended to make his last will, he answered with apostolic simplicity—"God knows, out of all my revenues, I have not a single coin to bequeath."—T. D. McGee's *History of Ireland.*

not unite in these enterprises. But a people so circumstanced have never united against an invader. They were half soldiers, half shepherds, living in clans, subject to chiefs of their own name and blood, and caring little for any other authority. They lived indeed much as the same race lived in the Scottish Highlands till the reign of George III. The jealousy of septs and the rivalry of chiefs prevented a national union, as similar jealousy had prevented the Britons from uniting in a national resistance to the Saxons, as similar jealousy divided the Highland clans into two hostile factions twenty generations later, when a prince of their own blood took the field at Prestonpans. The patriotism which combines in its sympathy the entire *patria*, was ill understood in rude ages by men of any race or clime. The chiefs of subjugated Gaul served in the legions of Cæsar, the Saxons fought under the banner of the Plantagenets, and the Cid with the most renowned Christian Knights of Spain sometimes took service with the Moors. The invaders themselves yielded to the spirit of the age, and were soon divided by as fierce jealousies as the Celtic chiefs. Norman barons made war on each other on the slightest occasion, and in the end made war on the king under whom they held. Nevertheless some generous English historians can recognise in resistance, continuing through so many generations in Ireland, only a turbulence and discontent native to the Celtic race. In the case of any other country they would probably find no insuperable difficulty in understanding why the dominion of strangers was odious, or why the desire to overthrow it was regarded as honourable and praiseworthy.*

It would have been a blessing to Ireland if the resistance had been successful; a blessing even if the conquest had been consummated as it was consummated in England and France. But it was her unhappy destiny to obtain neither the advantages of peace nor of war. Outside the Pale an Irish chief no more regarded a Plantagenet or a Tudor as his lawful sovereign than a Highland chief in later ages so regarded a Stuart or a Guelph: but it is certain

---

* The Saxons harassed the Norman conquerors by less legitimate methods, but one may learn from the triumphant tone in which Lord Macaulay tells the story, that to trouble a foreign invader in England was meritorious, even when it was hopeless to expel him.

"Some bold men, the favourite heroes of our oldest ballads, betook themselves to the woods and there in defiance of curfew laws and forest laws waged a predatory war against their oppressors. Assassination was an event of daily occurrence. Many Normans suddenly disappeared leaving no trace. The corpses of many were found bearing the marks of violence. Death by torture was denounced against the murderers, and strict search was made for them, but generally in vain; for the whole nation was in a conspiracy to screen them."—Macaulay's *England.*

The feuds of the Anglo-Normans are commonly accounted for in English History by the suggestion that the Barons were tainted with the contagious manners of the natives—an hypothesis which will scarcely account for the fact that more fierce and bloody wars were maintained on the soil of England by their kinsmen at home at a later period, during the Wars of the Roses.

that the chiefs living on the borders of the Pale would have made peace if they had been permitted to do so. They had a warning constantly under their eyes of the fate that awaited them if they did not, which the dullest could not misunderstand. "When the Pale was first planted, all the natives were expelled, so as not one Irish family had so much as one acre of freehold in all the five counties of the Pale."† In the reign of Edward I., and again in the reign of Edward III., they petitioned to be admitted to the benefit of English law and were refused. The Normans who fought for empire commonly respected the customs of a conquered race, and speedily incorporated them into their dominion; and a similar policy would have satisfied the general design of the politic Norman kings of England. But it has always been their fate in Ireland to lie at the mercy of their agents. The managers of the English interest, the officials of the Pale, "the Undertakers," as they were called in later times, wanted estates for themselves, and any policy which interfered with this purpose was thwarted or reversed. Had the chiefs become feudatories of the king there would be no longer any pretence for harassing them with military expeditions and seizing their lands as the spoil of battle. They accord-

---

† Sir John Davies.

ingly advised (in the interest of the natives of course; it was always the interest of the natives an English adventurer had on his lips when he was perpetrating what in modern times is called a job), that "the Irishery might not be naturalised without damage or prejudice *to themselves* or to the Crown," and this advice was accepted. It was a struggle not for supremacy but for the soil; and it went on, as we shall see, under varying conditions, for more than twenty generations.*

---

* Mr. Froude in his book on the English in Ireland (Vol. I., page 13), affirms that "everything which she most valued for herself—her laws and liberties, her orderly and settled government, the most ample security for person and property, England's first desire was to give to Ireland in fullest measure."

For this statement I cannot find the least foundation in history. It might be alleged with equal truth that the first desire of the British Parliament was to give the Jews in fullest measure the benefit of the British Constitution, but that no Hebrew could be induced to enter Parliament till the middle of the nineteenth century; or that the passionate longing of the Universities of Oxford and Cambridge to open their doors to Dissenters was baffled and thwarted by Nonconformist obstinacy till about the same era. To cite evidence on this point is an affront to good sense and educated opinion; but as Irish history is a blank to many otherwise well-informed persons, I venture to make an extract from Sir John Davies (Attorney-General of James I. in Ireland, and an Englishman), on the identical question. "This then I note as a great defect in the civil policy of this kingdom, in that for the space of 350 years at least after the conquest first attempted, the English lawes were not communicated to the Irish, nor the benefit and protection thereof allowed unto them; though they earnestly desired and sought the same. For as long as they were out of the protection of the laws, so

When the adventurers got estates, those who secured the great prizes returned to England to enjoy their plunder in peace; and with them began the pernicious system of absentee proprietors. The Normans who held fiefs in France and England were compelled to elect in which country they would reside and perform the duties for which the fief was created; the second estate went to a distinct heir. In Ireland the practice of holding the land and not performing the duties continues to this day. The Normans who fixed their homes in Ireland naturally modified their policy. They desired to live in friendship with the natives, and even to protect them from new aggressors. The succeeding generation came to have some affection for the country and the people; they often took Irish wives, and their children were fostered in Irish families. Then their heirs spoke the native tongue, wore the national mantle and barret, called themselves by native names, cherished the legends and laws of the Celts; and when in turn they came to rule, entertained bards and Brehons, and desired to be no more than Irish chiefs. The great proprietors who lived in England, the new arrivals who in each reign

---

as every Englishman might oppress, spoyle and kill them without controulment, howe was it possible they should be other than outlawes and enemies to the crowne of England." And again—"Whereby it is manifest, that such as had the government of Ireland under the crown of England did intend to make a perpetual separation of enmity between the English and the Irish."

came in fresh swarms, as men visit a wreck on a neighbouring coast, in search of plunder, and the officials of the Pale hated these Old English—so they came to be called—as bitterly as they hated the natives. They could not invariably be relied on to promote the Lord Deputy's designs, they began to have some pride of country, and were not always ready to make war on their kith and kin in the interest of the Pale. To check these offences a law was passed in the time of Edward III., which peremptorily forbade these relations with the natives under penalty of forfeiture or death.* To speak the native tongue, to use an Irish name, to wear the Irish apparel, or to adopt any of the customs of the country—" anie guize or fashion of the Irish"—was punishable by loss of their entire lands ; but to marry an Irishwoman, to entrust their children to an Irish nurse, or give them Irish sponsors at baptism—these grave offences were declared high treason. All men of Irish blood were forbidden to reside within a walled town, and, lest the Celts should obtain influence in a powerful spiritual confederacy, no native was to be received as a postulant in any monastery within the Pale. "Wilde Irish," who having been robbed of their lands sometimes wandered about the country houseless and desperate, were effectually restrained from renewing this grave offence.

---

* Statute of Kilkenny, A.D. 1366.

It was declared to "be lawful to all manner of men that find any thieves . . . [all manner of men being competent at once to detect thieves at sight] having no faithful men of good name and fame in their company, in English apparel, to take and kill those, and to cut off their heads."

Later critics affirm that strong measures were justified because the native customs were such as good policy required to be suppressed. For example, the land belonged under the Brehon law, not to the chief but to the sept; a custom which was highly inconvenient, to those who meditated confiscating it. Manslaughter was punished by an *eric* (or fine) levied off the offender and his kinsmen, instead of by the natural and legitimate method of strangulation. A race among whom capital punishment was unknown manifestly deserved no consideration; a money penalty for such a crime was a clear proof of barbarism, for obviously it is only the honour of women and the peace of families which may properly be made the subject of a judicial tariff. Another offence to right feeling was their national festival, derived from Pagan times, an assembly in the open air, and at a later period in the hall of the native chief or the Norman baron, where they listened to the songs of bards and the tales of *seanachies*, and witnessed feats of arms. This simple enjoyment a recent critic graciously compares to a *corroborie* of Maories.

It might be pleaded, perhaps that it was at such a *corroborie* the father of epic poetry sang the wrath of Achilles, and the wanderings of Ulysses; but let us rather admit the offence, and beseech the critic to make allowance for the rudeness of the age. It needed nearly seven centuries more to attain to the flower of civilised recreation in the Music Hall and the prize ring.

If the statesmen of the Pale taught the natives the use of the gallows it must be admitted that they placed the employment of it under salutary rules. An Irishman who murdered or maimed an Englishman was of course hanged, notwithstanding the law of Eric. But the killing of a native by an Englishman, even in time of peace, was no offence in the eye of the law; it was sufficient answer to the charge to plead that the murdered man was "a mere Irishman." The goods of a native might be taken at discretion, as he could not maintain an action in any court appointed by the Crown. But there were worse wrongs than these. Thomas Moore cites a case which makes the pulse of an Irishman throb with wrath, six centuries after the event. "Robert de la Roche and Adam le Waleys were indicted for an offence of this description (violation) against Margery O'Rorke; but it being found that the aforesaid Margery was an Irishwoman, the aggressors were acquitted." It is proper to note that from the time of Henry II., a gracious exception was made in favour of five families, one from each great division of the country, the O'Neills of Ulster, the O'Connors of Connaught, the O'Briens of Thomond, the O'Melachlins of Meath, and the MacMurroughs of Leinster (who had earned the favour by such worthy services). If a man could prove that he belonged to any of the "five bloods," he had an audience in an English court; otherwise not.* In official language, in all orders in Council, and Acts of Parliament the natives for ten generations and upwards were described as the "Irish enemy"—a phrase which implies all the licence of open warfare.

The Irish peasant is said to be lazy at home: he is confessedly industrious and enterprising in every other country where he has found a footing. It is proper to

---

* These are the facts which the annals of the period place beyond controversy. One may read in Mr. Froude, who apparently dreams his facts, that the conquerors strove painfully "to extend the forms of English liberty, her trial by jury, her local courts, her parliament, to the Irish people." Sir John Davies, who it may be presumed knew more of the matter, says—"But perhaps the Irish in former times did wilfully *refuse* to be subject to the laws of England, and would not be partakers of the benefit thereof, though the Crown of England did desire it; and therefore they were reputed aliens, outlaws and enemies? Assuredly the contrary does appear. . . . The mere Irish were not only accounted aliens, but enemies, and altogether out of the protection of the law; so as it was no capital offence to kill them: and this is manifest by many records. . . . For by divers heavy penal laws, the English were forbidden to marry, to foster, to make gossips with the Irish, or to have any trade or commerce in their markets or fairs."

note that the government of the Lord Deputy in those days laid the foundation of this habit, by a practice which would have destroyed industry among the Dutch or the Chinese. Soldiers were quartered on any district at the discretion of their officers, with the right of exacting whatever they required, without limit and without payment. An Anglo-Irish writer has described the effect on the people. "Their properties, their lives, the chastity of their families were all exposed to barbarians who sought only to glut their brutal passions; and by their horrible excesses purchased the curse of God and man."* And an Attorney-General, of English birth, notes the necessary result. "For when the husbandman had laboured all the yeare, the soldier in one night did consume the fruites of all his labour, *longique perit labor irritus anni.* Had hee reason then to manure the lande for the next yeare?"†

A detail of the excursions and achievements of English or Irish leaders which left no permanent result behind, does not fall within the design of this sketch. But there are transactions throwing light on the character of our ancestors, and of their enemies, with which the briefest history can scarcely dispense. When Robert Bruce was struggling for the deliverance of Scotland from English authority, he

---

* Leland's *History of Ireland.* Dr. Leland was a Fellow of Trinity College, and Chaplain to the Lord Lieutenant.
† Sir John Davies' Discourses.

was forced in an interval of ill fortune to fly to Ireland.
He was received with cordial welcome and hospitality in
Tir-Owen, and Irish allies accompanied him on his return,
and fought beside him at the decisive battle of Bannock-
burn. At this time John O'Neill was prince of Ulster;
his father had been elected Ardreigh, and he might hope
to attain to the same dignity himself, but he was persuaded that the North and South would not unite under
any native prince, and he had the magnanimity to propose
resigning his right in favour of Edward Bruce, the brother
of the Scottish king, provided that monarch came to the
help of Ireland. Bruce accepted the proposal, and speedily
sent over his brother with a force of six thousand men.
O'Neill and other Ulster chiefs joined him, and later
O'Connor of Connaught and O'Brien of Thomond with
their adherents. The whole of Ulster yielded to O'Neill
and Bruce, and they marched to Dundalk, within the
English Pale, and there proclaimed Edward King of Ireland. Unlike his wise brother the new king was self-
willed and impolitic; his countrymen had suffered grievous
wrongs from the English, and he made merciless reprisals
in Ireland; and sometimes on critical occasions he disre-
garded the advice of his native counsellors on questions
where the natives were necessarily the best judges. But
notwithstanding many errors his cause prospered. More
than half of the Irish chiefs, and the bulk of the native

clergy finally accepted him as their sovereign. He penetrated into the South, and when his brother came to his aid with a considerable army was able to march without resistance to the very walls of Dublin. It seemed at last that he had established himself securely in his new dominion, and Robert returned to Scotland.

The English ecclesiastics were his fiercest enemies'; they used the authority of their office, without stint, to inflame the adherents of the Lord Deputy against him, and by their advice, as seems probable, the English king (Edward I.) appealed to the Pope to persuade the native clergy to abandon his party. In answer to some remonstrance from Rome, John O'Neill undertook the vindication of his race. His letter to Pope John XXII. is one of the most remarkable state papers in the records of Ireland. "Before the coming of the stranger," he said, "we
" had a written code of laws according to which our nation
" was governed; they have deprived us of those laws, and
" of every law except one, which it is impossible to wrest
" from us; and for the purpose of exterminating us they
" have established iniquitous laws, by which injustice and
" inhumanity are combined for our destruction. Some of
" which we here insert for your inspection, as being so
" many fundamental rules of English jurisprudence estab-
" lished in this kingdom:—

"Every man not an Irishman, can on any charge, how-

"ever frivolous, prosecute an Irishman; but no Irishman,
"whether lay or ecclesiastic (the prelates alone excepted),
"can prosecute for any offence whatsoever, because he is
"an Irishman. If any Englishman should, as they often
"do, treacherously and perfidiously murder an Irishman,
"be he ever so noble or so innocent, whether lay or eccle-
"siastic, secular or regular, even though he should be a
"prelate, no satisfaction can be obtained from an English
"court of justice; on the contrary, the more worthy the
"murthered man was, and the more respected by his own
"countrymen, the more the murderer is rewarded and
"honoured; not only by the English rabble, but even by
"the English clergy and bishops; and especially by those,
"whose duty it is chiefly, on account of their station in life,
"to correct such abominable malefactors. Every Irish-
"woman, whether noble or ignoble, who marries an
"Englishman, is after her husband's death deprived
"of the third of her husband's lands and possessions, on
"account of her being an Irishwoman. In like manner,
"whenever the English can violently oppress to
"death an Irishman, they will by no means permit
"him to make a will or any disposal whatsoever of
"his affairs; on the contrary, they seize violently on all
"his property, deprive the Church of its rights, and per-
"force reduce to a servile condition that blood which has
"been from all antiquity free."

"They oblige us by open force," continues the Ulster Prince, "to give up to them our houses and our lands, and to seek shelter like wild beasts upon the mountains, in woods, marshes, and caves. Even there we are not secure against their fury; they even envy us those dreary and terrible abodes; they are incessant and unremitting in their pursuit after us; endeavouring to chase us from among them; they lay claim to every place in which they can discover us with unwarranted audacity and injustice; they allege that the whole kingdom belongs to them, and that an Irishman has no longer a right to remain in his own country."

"Let no person wonder then," he adds, in a document too long to be copied in its entirety, "if we endeavour to preserve our lives and defend our liberties, as well as we can, against those cruel tyrants, usurpers of our just properties and murderers of our persons; so far from thinking it unlawful, we hold it to be a meritorious act, nor can we be accused of perjury or rebellion, since neither our fathers or we, did at any time bind ourselves by any oath of allegiance to their fathers or to them, and therefore, without the least remorse of conscience, while breath remains, we will attack them in defence of our just rights, and never lay down our arms until we force them to desist."*

---

* This letter, according to the practice of the age, was written in

But the cause was to be decided not before the chair of Peter, but before the God of battles. The new king alienated many of the chiefs by wilfulness and perversity, and by these faults, in the end, his final ruin was wrought. The Lord Deputy, having received reinforcements from England, prepared for a decisive encounter with Bruce at Dundalk. Edward's brother, the King of the Scots, had again landed in Ireland with an auxiliary force, and was on his march to join him. The native chiefs advised him to defer the battle till the arrival of these reinforcements, but Edward, jealous, it is alleged, of his brother's renown, decided to fight at once. It was a fatal decision. He was defeated and slain in a great battle on Foughart Hill. His brother immediately returned to Scotland, and the war was at an end.* Foughart, like Crecy and Agincourt, and so many battles of the era, was won by skill and discipline against the headlong valour, contemptuous of the art of war, which delighted to call itself chivalry, and was often an insensate passion for personal distinction.

From this time forth the Norman kings had much at heart the design to win, or break, Ireland to complete sub-

---

Latin; I have taken the translation in the Appendix to Plowden's "Historical Review."

* Compacts and alliances between the two peoples were, however, renewed from time to time; and down to the reign of Henry VIII. we hear of the "Irish Skottes" as troublesome to the Pale.

mission. Edward III. asked the advice of his Irish counsellors whether the natives who were willing to accept the English law might not with advantage be received into grace as good subjects, paying of course a liberal fine to his exchequer for the favour. But the Irish counsellors, generally the latest arrivals from England who wanted estates, assured him the thing was impossible ; his true policy was to scourge the Irish, and to discipline "the degenerate English," as the natives of English blood were commonly called. The great Barons whose demesnes had been constituted palatines, engrossed, it was alleged, two-thirds of the country which submitted to the crown ; within which they made knights, created courts for civil and criminal causes, and entered into alliance and treaties with the Irish chiefs at their proper pleasure and irrespective of the king's wishes or interest. They were declared to be more Irish than the Irish themselves—a sentiment which meant not that they were more patriotic and national, but that they were more barbarous and troublesome than the natives. A Lord Lieutenant in those days was a powerful courtier who was allowed to plunder Ireland, often without taking the trouble to visit it ; sometimes one of the great absentees who drew immense incomes from the country and performed none of the duties for which his lands had been granted. His Lord Deputy was a soldier of fortune who went to Ireland, as other soldiers of fortune have gone to India, to enrich himself at the cost of the natives. It naturally happened that many of them were recalled, and cast into prison, and that some lost their heads for being in too great haste to grow rich, and too little mindful of the interest of their master. Sometimes the experiment was made of entrusting the office to the Earl of Desmond, or the Earl of Kildare, chiefs of the great Anglo-Norman family of Fitzgerald; but they were watched with constant suspicion, and generally ended their official career in the Tower of London; sometimes to a Lord Ormond, chief of the rival family of the Butlers, who were more circumspect or more selfish, and managed better to preserve the favour of the Court.

To make a hosting into the land bordering the Pale was a common pastime with a new Lord Deputy. When his trumpet was heard the strong took to their arms as resolute men do when they know a robber is in their house; and the weak fled to the mountains or the morasses, trusting to them rather than the vicegerent of the king. To intercept inconvenient complaints, a Lord Deputy caused a law to be passed which provided that anyone attempting to visit England without special license under the great seal should forfeit all his goods and chattels; and to ensure a vigilant watch over discontented persons it was ordered that half the penalty should go to the informer. Another Lord Deputy, when the Irish parliament agreed to a series of charges against him to be laid before the king, peremptorily refused the persons appointed to carry them to London permission to quit the country. But parliaments were not often so troublesome. They were held in those centuries wherever local convenience required, at Dublin or Drogheda, Kilkenny or Kells, and were for the most part submissive instruments of the Executive. There is not to be found in any act of parliament or ordinance made in Ireland in the middle ages the least suggestion that the natives had any right or duty except to enrich the invaders. An English bishop probably expressed the common consensus of his race when he brought a complaint before the House of Lords that an Archbishop of Cashel was filling his parishes with Irish ecclesiastics to the exclusion of Englishmen, and had even advised other bishops to take the same perverse course. It was on counsellors like these Edward had to rely, and he resolved to take decisive measures in the direction they suggested. He sent his son the Duke of Clarence into Ireland with orders that thenceforth no public employment should be exercised by any Irishman, whether of English or Irish blood. In a letter to the Lord Justiciary he laid down this policy with a plainness which is greatly to be preferred to the ingenious contrivances for disguising the same sentiment employed in later times:—

"Whereas it appeareth to us and our council, for many

" reasons that our service shall the better and more profit-
" ably be conducted in the said land by English officers
" having revenues and possessions in England, than by Irish
" or Englishmen married and estated in Ireland, and without
" any possessions in our realm of England ; we enjoin you
" that you diligently inform yourself of all our officers
" greater or lesser within our land of Ireland aforesaid;
" and that all such officers beneficed, married and estated
" in the said land, and having nothing in England, be
" removed from their offices; that you place and substitute
" in their room other fit Englishmen, having lands, tene-
" ments, and benefices in England, and that you cause the
" said offices for the future to be executed by such English-
" men, and none other, any order of ours to you made
" in contrarywise notwithstanding."

The Celts were of course more decisively dealt with ; in their case it was ordered by royal mandate that " no mere " Irishman should be admitted into any office or trust in " any city, borough, or castle, in the king's land : that no " bishop or prior, under the king's dominion and allegiance " should admit any of this race to an ecclesiastical benefice, " or into any religious house, on account of consanguinity, " or other pretence whatever." They were forbidden to reside within a walled town or even to visit one on business.* To give permanence to this policy, a

* To evade and defeat this prohibition became a point of honour. The

statute was passed to separate the two nations for ever—the statute of Kilkenny, already described.* And that nothing might be wanting to complete success, the English bishops in Ireland denounced the terrible penalty of excommunication upon any one who should presume to violate this new law. The Duke of Clarence, then Lord Lieutenant at Dublin, devised a scheme worthy to crown and consummate the good work. He advised that one or more families should be sent into Ireland from every parish in England, to replace the natives. Though it proved impossible at the moment to act on this practical suggestion, it only waited for a more convenient opportunity.†

Irish annalists tell how the weak places in the castles and towns of the Pale were detected by Donough Fitzpatrick, son of the Lord of Ossory, a patriot spy. A native poet describes his disguises and metamorphoses with cordial enjoyment :—

"He is a carpenter, he is a turner,
"My nursling is a bookman,
"He is selling wine and hides
"Wheresoever he sees a gathering."

* See *ante* p. 29.
† England became prosperous and powerful because her Norman conquerors were gradually compelled to abandon their connexion with France, and become Englishmen. Ireland would have perhaps prospered on the same condition. If the Geraldines and Butlers, the Burkes and Barnwells had been permitted to follow their inclination and become Irishmen, England, after a little would have been to them no more than France was to their kinsmen at Westminster, and the Normans of Irish

Those who cannot have peace can at least have war. The natives naturally flew to arms. Several descendants of Dermid MacMurrough at various intervals had fought against the English, their patriotism being stimulated, it is to be feared, by the circumstance that when Dermid died Strongbow cheated them out of their tribal lands. But there was now a chief of the race who loved and served his country for its own sake. Art Kavanagh, whose territory, it was complained, " lay like a cancer on the heart of Leinster," defeated the king's son at Kilmainham, and chased him to the gates of Dublin. It was but one of many achievements. Art enjoyed a reign of more than average length, distinguished by more than ordinary success, and lived and died an implacable enemy of the stranger. At a later date O'Brien of Thomond followed his example with notable success; and other chiefs of less distinguished lineage still pressed upon the receding Pale. Castle after castle pulled down the banner of St. George, till in the reign of Henry VII. little remained under English authority but Dublin and its precincts. Many of the Anglo-Norman barons only maintained their position by alliances with the native chiefs, or by paying an ignominious tribute for their protection,

---

birth would have finally merged into one nation with the Celt as the Normans of English birth merged into one nation with the Saxon.

known in Anglo-Irish records as the Black Rent.* In these emergencies the English kings made spasmodic efforts to compel the great proprietors, who were habitual absentees, to bear some share of the burthen of defending their own interests. Under Richard II. they were taxed for a time to the extent of two-thirds of their revenue; at a later date their estates were declared forfeited, if, within a given time, they did not personally occupy and defend them.† But they were too strong at Westminster not to

---

* The State Papers of the succeeding reign enumerates the sum paid as Black Rent in the time of Henry VIII.

"Here followeth the names of the English counties that bear tribute to the wylde Irish:—

"The barony of Leechahill in the county of Wolster, to the captain of Clanhuboy, payeth yearly £40; or else to Oneyll, whether of them be strongest. The county of Uryell payeth yearly to the great Oneyll, £40. The county of Meathe payeth yearly to O'Conor, £300. The county of Kyldare payeth yearly to the said O'Conor, £20. The King's Exchequer payeth yearly to M'Morough 80 marks. The county of Wexford payeth yearly to M'Morough and to Arte Oboy, £40. The county of Kilkenny and the county of Tipperary pay yearly to O'Carroll, £40. The county of Limerick payeth yearly to O'Brien Arraghe, in English money, £40. The same county of Limerick payeth yearly to the great O'Brien, in English money, £40. The county of Cork to Cormac M'Teyge payeth yearly in English money, £40. Summa, £740."

† The absentees ran a still narrower chance than this. In the Wars of the Roses the Irish Barons were partizans of the House of York, and received with enthusiasm famous impostors (Perkin Warbeck and Simnel Lambert), trained to personate chiefs of that party. One of the parliaments called in this interest in Dublin is memorable for a declaration of rights which anticipated by more than three centuries the

thwart and defeat these attempts, which were finally relinquished as hopeless. Down to this day these great proprietors have ruled Ireland at their pleasure; not for its benefit, not even for the benefit of England, but to preserve and increase the revenues which they draw from confiscated estates.

In the reign of Henry VII. there was little leisure at court for Irish affairs, but it is a reign rendered memorable by one transaction. That subtle king pushed the submission of the Pale parliament and the Pale garrison to the last extremity of human baseness. A Deputy named Sir Edward Poyning obtained from them acts by which it was directed that the judges and all persons concerned in the administration of justice should no longer hold by patents for life, but only during the king's pleasure; that no one not of English birth should be entrusted with any

---

nationality preached by Swift and Molyneux, and established by Grattan. In 1452 they declared that henceforth Ireland must be governed by its own laws and customs, and by the Lords and Commons of the land in parliament assembled; that no one summoned into England to answer before a foreign jurisdiction should be bound to obey the summons; and that any officers putting writs for this purpose into execution should forfeit their goods and chattels. And with respect to the estates of habitual absentees, this parliament declared them forfeited by the continuous neglect of the service for which they were granted. But all the acts passed in the time of the "Lad," were disallowed in England, and this one among the rest, though they were nearly the only acts worth preserving.

place of strength within the settlement, and that no parliament should be held for the future till the king's lieutenant and council in Ireland had certified to him the causes and considerations for holding it, and transmitted a schedule of all such acts as they considered should be passed in it; and this schedule must be sanctioned by the king and his council (in London), and his license under the great seal (of England) obtained, before such parliament could be summoned. Any parliament held contrary to the form and provisions so framed to be void and of none effect in law. That Anglo-Normans submitted to this system is a puzzle to modern critics. It was the air of Ireland, an ingenious commentator suggests, which induced men of British descent to endure such a bondage. The contagion in that case must have crossed the sea at Donaghadee, for in Scotland under the Stuarts no Bill could be submitted to parliament till it had been approved by the Lords of Articles, and in the parliaments which dealt with it no Presbyterian had a seat.

The king, so successful with his lieges, made small head against native discontent; and in the succeeding reign, when Henry VIII. was jousting in the Field of the Cloth of Gold within the English Pale in France, the English Pale in Ireland, which had once embraced six counties, and stretched its offshoots deep into the South and deep into the North, was reduced to a territory which might be conveniently inspected in a morning ride from Dublin Castle.

The Reformation suddenly changed the condition of the contest, and the parties to it. The English Crown which claimed the Lordship of Ireland under the authority of the Pope, and for certain services to be performed at his instance, was now at war with the Sovereign Pontiff, and might be considered to have forfeited its original title. Only two reigns earlier the grant of Adrian IV. was recited in an Act of Parliament as the sole foundation of English authority.* The little parliament of the Pale, consisting chiefly of servants of the Crown, when they became possessed of the king's wishes, however, were as willing to gratify them as his parliament in London had proved. They invested Henry with the first fruits of bishopricks, abbeys, hospitals, and colleges, and the absolute property of certain religious houses which he proposed to confiscate for his personal profit, and, after a little, they barred the Pope's title by declaring Henry King of Ireland, and not

---

* "Whereas our holy father, Adrian, Pope of Rome, was possessed of all the signiory of Ireland, in right of his Church, which for a certain rent he alienated to the King of England and his heirs for ever; by which grant the subjects of Ireland owe their obedience to the King of England, as their sovereign lord; it is therefore ordained that all archbishops and bishops of Ireland, shall, upon the monition of forty days, proceed to the excommunication of all disobedient subjects; and if such archbishop or bishop be remiss in doing their duties in the premises, they shall forfeit one hundred pounds."—Edw. IV., 1467.

merely Lord Paramount as theretofore. In his domestic affairs they were equally accommodating. They pronounced his marriage with Catharine of Arragon null and void, and that the inheritance of the crown rightfully descended through the heirs of Queen Anne (Anne Boleyn); to question which descent at any time thereafter was declared high treason. But Henry was a sovereign with whose imperious will the most obedient parliament could scarce keep pace. These acts had barely become law when the news arrived that he had caused Queen Anne to be tried, condemned and executed, and had married another lady. The Pale parliament immediately repealed their original acts, and passed another attainting Anne, and declaring the heirs of the new wife to be entitled to the throne; with the usual penalties against all malevolent persons who should not change their minds with equal expedition.

In England Henry claimed to possess and exercise all the spiritual authority which had belonged to the Pope; which for a sovereign who had so many troublesome cases of conscience to solve, was manifestly a convenient arrangement. He was encouraged by courtly ecclesiastics, who outran him in exalting the royal prerogative, and reducing archbishops and bishops to the condition of servitors, nominated and removable at pleasure. He had to encounter resistance from some of the great English nobles, and to face two insurrections of the people, but a still increasing number of his English subjects, and finally the bulk of the nation, acquiesced in his claims, and allowed him to proclaim himself head of the Church, with little more scruple than the Roman populace felt in accepting Cæsar as Pontifex Maximus. In Ireland also the parliament acknowledged him as their spiritual head; and, indeed, followed him rejoicingly through the long series of marriage feasts which he celebrated with perplexing rapidity; not, as an eminent historian assures us, for any base personal gratification, but purely for the welfare of England which wanted an heir to so many virtues.

The officials of the Pale might pleasure his Highness, but the Irish and the old English were of a different temper. He could call himself king if he thought proper, but his pretension to determine such inflammatory questions as the mass, the sacraments, and the primacy of the Holy See, the bulk of neither race would tolerate. Strange stories of Henry's levity and cruelty, of his plunder of religious houses, and of his ill-regulated passion for new wives and new opinions, came across the channel; and we may well believe that when this strange claim was canvassed at the board, or announced from the altar, it was heard with some such mixture of contempt and horror as the pretensions of Mormonism excited in our own day among a people less prone than the Irish to reverence or enthusiasm.*

The manner in which the great moral revolution was carried out in Ireland was not calculated to edify a religious people. "They broke down the monasteries (says the Annals of the Four Masters) and sold their roofs and bells, from Aran of the Saints to the Iccian Sea!" "They burned the images, shrines, and relics of the saints; they destroyed the Statue of our Lady of Trim, and the Staff of Jesus, which had been in the hand of St. Patrick!"

After the brief reign of Edward VI. the throne once again was filled by a Catholic Sovereign.† She employed

---

* This is not the last judgment pronounced on the subject. Writers of great authority in our own time (Messrs. Carlyle and Froude) declare that the Irish ought to have accepted the Reformation, and that they have been justly punished by all that ensued for their perversity in refusing to accept it. Our deference to the opinion of these eminent persons on the point is disturbed by a doubt whether, after two centuries and a half further experience, they accept a tittle of it themselves, or regard the authority of Henry and Cranmer with any more respect, at bottom, than the authority of Joe Smith and Orson Pratt.

† There was a short struggle in Edward's reign between the Lord Deputy and certain native chiefs, conducted in a characteristic manner. O'Moore and O'Connor had risen to resist a private wrong, and being unsupported were not successful. Certain English officers advised them to throw themselves on the mercy of the young king; even his stern father, they suggested, had cheerfully accepted the submission of chiefs willing to make their peace, and had restored them to their lands and offices. They submitted, and went into England accordingly, where they were immediately thrown into prison, and their lands divided among the

herself hanging and burning the followers of the new faith,
as her father had hanged and burned the followers of the
old one. In Dublin the Catholics were restored to power,
and used their authority with singular forbearance. It is
a fact which stands alone in the history of that troubled
century in Europe, that during the whole reign, no Protestant in Ireland suffered death for his opinions. On the
contrary English Protestants flying from the persecution
at home were sheltered in Dublin from all molestation.*
But so little did religion modify the fundamental relations
between the countries, that Catholic Mary and Catholic
Philip confiscated the native lands in a wide district of
Leinster, which still retains the names of the Queen's
County and the King's County in memory of that transaction. The energetic queen would have extirpated
the population also but for the intercession of the Catholic
Primate. Their territory it was said had been made a
highway to Munster by ill-disposed persons; if so, they
were, of course, justly punished; for what business had
their lands to lie in a place which prejudiced " the

---

identical advisers who had proffered them this friendly counsel. O'Moore
died in prison, where O'Connor would probably have died also, but that a
new reign brought about his release.

*And as it thus escaped the effects of Mary's diabolical rancour,
several English families friends to the Reformation, fled into Ireland, and
there enjoyed their opinions and worship in privacy, without notice or
molestation. (Leland's *History of Ireland.*)

interest of the queen's majestie." The confiscated districts she planted largely with English settlers, and had an act passed to facilitate plantation for the future. The spiritual system established by Henry and Edward of course disappeared, and the entire nation returned to Catholic worship and practices. But the innovations by which the temporal authority of the Sovereign had been enlarged were maintained in full force. She held a fast grasp of the lands taken from the suppressed monasteries, and continued to make grants of them at her discretion, in the interval of burning her English subjects for disputing the authority of the Church which she robbed. Mary has left an odious reputation; and the horror excited by her cruelties is made a reproach, to this day, against the only people who having power did not imitate them.

Of the Pale parliament it is scarcely necessary to say that they duly enacted (anything to the contrary theretofore ordered nevertheless, notwithstanding) that her majesty, having been born in wedlock, the succession belonged of right to her, and to her heirs; and they promptly repealed all the laws they had formerly made in favour of Edward. On this occasion the *dramatis personæ* were somewhat different, but veterans could be found who had travelled unshrinkingly the whole round of royal dubitation from Henry to Mary.

The religious quarrel smouldered, or only broke out in

turmoils till the time of Elizabeth. Laws had been made to compel conformity, but they were ill-enforced; preachers of the new creed were appointed to convert the people, but they clung to the Pale and the strong towns, which Henry, as we have seen, knew how to convert without their assistance. Elizabeth, however, determined that all Ireland must be brought to submission, and two wars of unprecedented fierceness and duration were the result.

Before war the politic princess however tried diplomacy. The most dangerous chiefs were pacified with unstinted promises. Shane O'Neill, Prince of Ulster, known in native annals as John the Proud, having marched into the Pale at the head of a formidable force, found himself, after a little, recognised by the Lord Deputy as the O'Neill, with the like jurisdiction, authority, and pre-eminence as his ancestors had enjoyed with that title, and even invited to visit London, and have a personal conference with her Highness. Shane went to England, and there was no Seanachie in Ulster but could tell afterwards what a gallant show his following made before the staring churls of Clan London; how boldly he bore himself among the strange lords, and how graciously he was received by the Queen. There may indeed be heard down to our own day, at wakes and weddings, any where between the Bann and the Culduff, strange traditions of the favours won by the tall Irish chief from the gracious Princess. The favours of queens are often perilous gifts. Elizabeth sent him away loaded with presents, and on his return he did her signal service by overthrowing an expedition of Scots into Ireland, and slaying its chief. But he was dangerously strong, and, in the end, paid the ordinary penalty. After his return to Tyrone the Lord Deputy acknowledged his services by a noble gift of wine, and even held out hopes of bestowing his sister in marriage on the ally and good friend of his royal mistress. The most intrepid vindicator of the English in Ireland admits that this wine was poisoned to make away with Shane, and that the lady, whom Irish seanachies believe to have been his royal mistress in more senses than one, was probably a party to the plot.* The brew was mingled with less than the

---

* "A present of wine was sent to Shane from Dublin. It was consumed at his table—but the poison had been unskilfully prepared. It brought him and half his household to the verge of death, but no one actually died. Refined chemical analysis was not required to detect the cause of the illness; and Shane clamoured for redress with the fierceness of a man accustomed rather to do wrong than to suffer it. The guilt could not be fixed on Sussex. The crime was traced to an English resident in Dublin named Smith; and if Sussex had been the instigator, his instrument was too faithful to betray him. Yet after the fatal letter in which the Earl had revealed to Elizabeth his own personal endeavours to procure O'Neill's murder, the suspicion cannot but cling to him that the second attempt had been made with his privity. Nor can Elizabeth herself be wholly acquitted of responsibility."—*Froude's* History of England, Vol. VIII., page 49.

ordinary skill of an official poisoner, and Shane escaped this time; but his enemies were unsleeping. After serious reverses he sought to make allies of the Scots whom he had defeated in the queen's interest; and at a feast which they made to welcome him, he was assassinated at the instigation of an English spy maintained in his territory by the Lord Deputy, who duly paid his agent a thousand marks from the public treasury for this good service. But first and last Tyrowen was an expensive acquisition. To encounter, placate, and finally subdue and murder Shane cost a sum enormous for that age, nearly half a million of money. Other chiefs less to be feared were persuaded to sit in the Pale parliament, and two O'Reillys of Cavan, a Macguiness of Down, an O'Brien of Clare, and two O'Farrells of Longford accepted the invitation. Sagacious rulers have never been ignorant that to encourage treason it is necessary to be profuse in rewards, and faithful in compacts, with traitors, and Elizabeth, it may be assumed, was ready to comply with this rule. But the "Undertakers" in Dublin regarded the interest of the Crown as a Nabob in the Carnatic regarded the interest of the East India Company, at a prodigious interval after their own, and the reign of this sagacious woman is marked by constant crimes of treachery and falsehood. The case of McMahon of Monaghan is still recalled in Ulster with rage and tears. He submitted to the crown and had his lands restored under the great seal of England with remainder to his brother. On his death this brother took possession, and the Lord Deputy visited his territory for the ostensible purpose of installing him on behalf of the crown. But some complaint—trumped up for the occasion it is alleged— having been made against McMahon that two years before he had collected certain over due rents by the aid of armed retainers, a practice nearly as common then as ejectment in our own day, the Lord Deputy tried him for this offence before a jury composed of common soldiers, hanged him on the spot, and divided his land among English adventurers, some of whom have enjoyed the revenues of the McMahon country from the date of that transaction down to our own day.* In the first instance a few fragments of the spoil were given to certain natives as a

---

* A district of this county fell to the lot of a lucky English adventurer who let it out to native tenants subject to an annual rent of between three and four hundred pounds. The tenants made themselves rude dwellings, lived in a rude fashion, and cultivated the soil with constant industry for the benefit of the new proprietor and his heirs. When I last saw the district, nearly thirty years ago, the people were dying of famine, the agent of a moiety of the property was amusing the English public with romances of the barbarity of a peasantry who would not starve without making a clamour, and the heirs of the lucky adventurer were drawing out of it five-and-twenty thousand pounds a year in rent to be spent in England. One may say with Robert Burns—
" ' Tis hardly in a body's power
To keep at times from being sour
To see how things are shared,"

placebo; but when they desired to enter on possession their claims were disposed of as summarily as the chief's. "Patk. M'Collo M'Bryen, coming upon safe conduct to the Parson O'Connellan, then justice of the peace, and chief man in authority for her Majesty in that county [to take possession of his allotment] was intercepted by an ambush appointed by the said Parson and Captain Willis, and there slain."* This was not a promising method of encouraging chiefs to make submission; but many English statesmen were of opinion that not submission and peace but conflict and confusion were the result to be desired in Ireland. Sir Henry Sidney, then Lord Deputy, in confidential correspondence with his royal mistress, reminds her of the language held by some of her counsellors, who have never wanted successors at Westminster:—

"Should we exert ourselves," said they, "in reducing
" this country to order and civility, it must soon acquire
" power, consequence, and riches, the inhabitants will be
" thus alienated from England; they will cast themselves
" into the arms of some foreign power, or perhaps erect
" themselves into an independent state. Let us rather
" connive at their disorders; for a weak and disordered
" people never can attempt to detach themselves from the
" crown of England." The middle class scarcely under-

---

* "Carew MS.," cited by Mr. Richey in his Trinity College "Lectures on Irish History."

stood the subtle policy of statesmen, but they arrived at the same end by methods of their own. It was only after unsuccessful insurrection, and unsuccessful negociation with Catholic Powers that they had submitted to the wishes of Henry VIII.; but from the moment they submitted they seem to have considered the resistance of Ireland as odious, if not unpardonable. A curious characteristic of England, throughout her wonderful history, is the wrath and scorn with which she regards any people who hold to-day an opinion which she held only yesterday.

But all questions of secular policy were lost in the great struggle for religious liberty, and never was contest among any people more purely for this principle. What the Irish sought was not to put down the new creed, but to secure for themselves the right of practising their own creed in peace. The Geraldines, the most powerful of the Anglo-Norman barons, took the field in Desmond, and were joined by the bulk of the native chiefs in that ancient territory, but they had no concert with the Irish princes in the north, who sat still and aided neither party. The most vigorous and capable of the O'Neills, indeed, Hugh or Aodh, who afterwards performed prodigies of labour and valour in the Irish cause, having been educated at London in the policy and religion of the queen, served at this time in the army of the Lord Deputy. The chiefs of Desmond maintained the contest with varying fortune for several years. The first English army was destroyed in two or three campaigns, but another was got on foot to take its place, and an expenditure, which for that age was enormous, incurred to equip it efficiently. Carew, a stern, skilful soldier, was the commander in Munster, and partly by successful fighting, partly by unscrupulous intrigue, of which also he was a master, brought the war to a close. How he improved his victory, in the interest of the Queen and the Church, may still be read in his own triumphant language in the *Pacata Hibernia.* If the Mohawks had chronicles they could scarce match the grim enjoyment with which the tale of horrors is told. Munster was known as the "Garden of Ireland." To comprehend the devastations inflicted on it the reader will have to recall the atrocities in Bulgaria over which humanity shuddered in our own day. Old and young, men and women, were butchered indiscriminately. "The blind and " feeble, boys and girls, sick persons, idiots and old people," are enumerated in the Irish annals as among the slain. Those whom the sword could not reach, were deliberately given a prey to famine. The cattle were everywhere killed or driven away into strong places, and the crops and houses delivered to the flames. One of Carew's lieutenants boasted that in a wide and fertile district, he had left neither horn nor corn nor house unburned. When every show of resistance ceased, the slaughter did not cease. It is still only by modern examples that the spirit and scope of this war of extermination can be understood. A French marshal in our day who stifled with smoke and fire a tribe of Arabs sheltering in a cavern, is denounced as a monster, but this device was repeatedly anticipated in the Desmond war by the soldiers of Elizabeth.* More men, women and children were killed by starvation in pursuance of the orders of the Lord President, when there was no longer an Irish soldier in arms, than perished in the three French revolutions by the crimes of the Jacobins, the Reds and the Communists. The persecution of English Protestants by Mary had been merciless, but Elizabeth murdered more Irish Catholics in a week in Munster, than Mary murdered English Protestants in her entire reign. Half the population of the island was destroyed, and Ireland was pro-

---

* A similar outrage, Sismondi relates, was committed at the siege of Vicenza in 1510, by a leader of mercenaries on a number of the inhabitants who concealed themselves in a subterranean quarry. Bayard, who was engaged in the siege, hearing of this proceeding hurried to the spot, and expressed his view of the transaction by immediately hanging two of the wretches who had lighted the fire! There was much need of a Bayard in Munster in the reign of Elizabeth. The nearest approach to a Bayard discernible in that day was otherwise engaged. A Spanish expedition sent in aid of the Irish, having capitulated at Smerwick on conditions, their native allies to the number of eight hundred were ordered to be slaughtered in cold blood, and one of the two officers charged with this duty was Sir Walter Raleigh. When he was hurried to death, by a thankless master, without a moment's pause for preparation, perhaps "the gallant Raleigh" remembered the massacre in Desmond.

nounced to be "pacified" as in later times "peace reigned in Warsaw."* To commemorate the victory the head of Desmond was exhibited to the applauding burghers of London, as the dead body of Sir William Wallace had been shown to their predecessors by Edward I.

Under the Tudors the assent of the sovereign was not a figure of speech; Elizabeth, the haughtiest and most exacting of a jealous race, personally scrutinised and sanctioned the measures adopted. She sent her thanks and even her blessing to her "faithful George," for his good services among the Munster Papists. Let the reader note how hard it is, even at this day, to harmonise the opinion of the two nations. These were the golden days of good Queen Bess, when the gallant Raleigh flourished as a type of adventurous chivalry, and Edmund Spenser

---

* A specimen or two of the *Pacata Hibernia* will suffice to indicate its character. An English expedition entered an Irish camp where, says the chronicler, "they found none but hurt and sick men, whose pains and lives by the soldiers were soon determined." "The President having received certaine information, that the Mounster fugitives were harboured in those parts, having before burned all the houses and corne, and taken great preyes in Owny Onubrian and Kilquig, a strong and fast countrey, not farre from Limerick, diverted his forces into East Clanwilliam and Muskeryquirke, where Pierce Lacy had lately beene succoured: and harassing the country, killed all mankind that were found therein, for a terrour to those as should give releefe to runagate traitors. Thence wee came into Arleaghe woods, where wee did the like, not leaving behind us man or beast, corne or cattle, except such as had been conveyed into castles."

was the greatest but one of the poets who have made the age illustrious. But the gallant Raleigh was in Munster during these transactions hunting for Irish lands; he got forty thousand acres of the Desmond confiscation, and paid for them by services worthy of Nana Sahib; and the poet who was in attendance on his patron to pick up the scraps and fragments, got also a scanty meal of forfeited lands; and rivalled Giraldus Cambrensis in eagerness to serve the adventurers, with the pen which wrote the Faery Queen.*
Of the daughters of Henry one has descended to posterity branded by the wrath of her subjects with the infamous title of the "bloody queen;" but it was not the lady who left Desmond without horn or corn or rooftree upstanding; she, we are taught, was the grace and glory of her age.

The Spaniards had given encouragement, and some insufficient aid in men and money, to the Desmonds; and when the sailing of the Armada with chiefs of the House of Desmond on board was reported in Ireland, it, doubtless,

---

* After describing scenes which he witnessed when the war was over, when the fugitives came creeping "out of every corner of the woods and glynnes on their hands, for their legges would not bear them," and for food "they did eate the dead carrion happy where they could finde them, yea and one another soon after"—the gentle Edmund proposes as a happy method of making an end of the race, much sooner than could be otherwise hoped for, that they should not be permitted to till their land or pasture their cattle next season, and thereupon he felt assured "they would quickly consume themselves and devour one another."

suggested hopes which were natural under the circumstances. The tempest which scattered the Armada cast seventeen ships of war on the coast of Ireland, where the Spaniards were received with hospitality and consideration due to men of the same race and creed. Some of the chiefs engaged in this work were too strong for immediate reprisals, but O'Rourke of Brefni had to fly from the vengeance of the Lord Deputy for his part in it. He threw himself on the hospitality of his other kinsmen the Scots, and the Scots (who had perhaps forgotten how Robert Bruce was received in Ireland in his day of danger) transmitted him to the court of Elizabeth, who ordered him to be executed. The head of an Irish chief at the Tower or on Temple Bar indeed was for many generations an ordinary recreation for the good citizens of London.

When the Desmond war was long finished and half a million of acres of forfeited land distributed among the successful soldiers, their camp-followers, and a new swarm of settlers from England,* the northern chiefs

---

* The device of the Duke of Clarence in Henry VII.'s reign was now employed. Letters were sent to every county in England to encourage young men of good family to become planters in Desmond; the land was offered at a nominal rent, on condition that they should accept no natives as tenants! A large settlement took place. It is to be noticed that some of the disaster of the famine created in Munster by Carew extended to the victorious party; a return is

renewed the contest on their own account. This time it
was the Celt who took the field, and the half of the island
which the former wars had scarcely reached was called to
arms. The leaders of the northern revolt were the
hereditary princes of Ulster, O'Neill and O'Donnell. When
they were mere youths the Queen's Government had made
each of these chieftains the subject of a separate experiment, which had equally failed. Hugh O'Neill, who was
not in the right line of succession to the chieftaincy but
near enough to make a convenient "Queen's O'Neill," was
brought to London, trained in the civil and military
learning of the period, converted to the religion of the
State, placed in the English army, and finally sent to Ireland to serve with the Queen's troops in the Desmond
War. For these and other services, not pleasant to recall,
he was created Earl of Tyrone, and taken into the special
favour of her Grace, who had a tenderness for handsome
young soldiers. But when Hugh settled down at Dungannon among his own race, and saw the seamy side of the
royal policy in Ireland, his sympathy with the Court cooled

---

quoted by Leland showing the prodigious prices to which provisions rose
in Dublin next season. Wheat from thirty-six shillings to nine pounds
the quarter; barley malt, from ten shillings to forty-three shillings the
barrel; pease, from five shillings to forty shillings the peck; beef from
twenty-six shillings and eight pence to eight pounds the carcase; mutton,
from three shillings to twenty-six shillings the carcase; a lamb, from
twelve pence to six shillings; a pork, from eight to thirty shillings.

E.

fast, quarrels arose, reproaches and menaces were exchanged, and after long delay and apparent hesitation Hugh took his stand plainly at the head of the party of resistance, and gave up both the policy and the creed he had been taught. Hugh O'Donnell had been dealt with in a different fashion, but one that proved in the upshot as unavailing. An English ship masquerading as a merchantman laden with Spanish wine, anchored on the coast of Lough Swilly in the O'Donnell's country; the young chieftain, then a boy, with his following were invited on board to taste the generous vintage of Xeres, and when they were carousing in the cabin, the sails were set and he was carried away to Dublin, and lodged a prisoner in the keep known as Birmingham Tower. After several years' imprisonment he escaped, and regained his native mountains, still under the age of manhood, but in excellent temper to join a revolt. He made peace with his hereditary rival O'Neill, and served loyally under him till his death.

O'Neill, who by age and capacity was the natural head of the confederacy, defeated the English in two great battles, and the whole of the north fell under his sway. He made a solemn appeal to the Anglo-Norman Catholics to come to his aid; reciting the wrongs inflicted on both races who had now at last, he insisted, a common cause. "Treaties have been violated; submissions received, with a shameful and contemptuous disregard to the most "solemn promises; our fortunes have been torn from us; "our consciences have been enslaved; but our oppressors, "not yet satiated, now prepare to exterminate the wretched "natives who have presumed to assert their liberty, and "thus to erect a tyrannical dominion even over those who "call themselves English subjects, and are so infatuated "as not to discern, that the present is the common cause "of all."

He marched into Munster, and the remnant of the Irish clans, still left after the Desmond massacre, joined him. Elizabeth sent Essex against him with a great force, but Essex accomplished nothing, and returned to London to disgrace and death. Philip of Spain, then the most powerful prince in Europe, sent him money and ammunition, with promises of more effectual help later. Envoys from Philip, from France, and from the Pope were in his camp, and his son was invited to Madrid to be educated in the arms and policy of the great empire. In the end an expedition from Spain came to his assistance, but too late to be of effectual help. England was served, at this time, by great statesmen, and one man, who for subtlety and unscrupulousness was a rival for the Italian of evil name who a little earlier taught tyrants that the art to rule successfully was to deceive, helped Elizabeth by a serviceable suggestion. Bacon recommended that she should try a "princelie policie of division"—that is to say the encouragement of chiefs to break faith with each other, and of clansmen to sell their chiefs for bribes. We hear of a Queen's O'Neill, a Queen's Tyrconnell, Maguire, O'Reilly, and so forth, set up as competitors to the legitimate chief chosen by the clan, as a consequence of this counsel. But the "princelie policie" had more humiliating results—a son of the Desmond executed in London, who had been bred in the religion of England, was taken out of the Tower, to rally South Munster for the queen, which he failed, ignominiously, to accomplish; but a brother and an illegitimate son of O'Neill himself, were caught in the snare, and might be found with many other traitors in the camp of Elizabeth. It is not without satisfaction that one reads of a skilful device of the Lord Deputy, communicated with great glee to the queen, for turning these distrusted partisans to advantage; they were always placed in the post of danger, so that whether they killed or were killed her majestie would be profited by the transaction. Forged letters were a common device to excite distrust; poisoned wine was used with the sanction of the Lord Deputy for getting rid of dangerous and incorruptible enemies; and, in short, Bacon's "princelie policie" proved as plentiful a source of evil as the teaching of Machiavelli. An English soldier who won renown and founded a family in Ireland in this era, commonly distinguised himself, when his achievements are closely inspected, by

a perfidy worthy of a Hindoo, supplemented by
ferocity worthy of a Mohawk.* Elizabeth, after a
reign of nearly half a century, at length drew near
her end; and it was considered of great importance to
close the Irish war before a Scotch king, or a disputed
succession, gave it new chances. O'Donnell had gone to
Spain for succours, but they were slow to come, and the
"princelie policie" had greatly thinned the ranks of the
Irish army. At length the Lord Deputy proposed terms,
which O'Neill deemed he could honourably accept. He
and his allies were taken into the Queen's favour, confirmed
in their possessions, and the free exercise of their religion
guaranteed to them. Hugh was to lay down his title of
the O'Neill, and content himself with that of Earl of
Tyrone, while O'Donnell, in lieu of his Celtic chieftaincy,

---

* The methods by which the English made war in Ireland in that era
may be judged from the admissions of their most vehement apologist in
our own day. In Mr. Froude's History of England we find the exploits
of an expedition sent into the O'Byrne country in Wicklow. The
narrative may teach Englishmen to be patient with Turks, Muscovites,
and Ojibeway Indians. "Feagh MacHugh, of whom they were chiefly
"in search, was absent, but 'they slew two of his foster brothers, four
"or five kerns, and as many others as were in five cabins.' This done
"they turned homewards. On their way they picked up a woman,
"whom Agard carried to the station, meaning, as he said, 'to execute
"her unless she would serve his purpose.' Captain George, with a
"scouting party, encountered a party of Tallows, who had been abroad
"at mischief. One of them was killed; the rest, as the soldiers wanted
"amusement, were stripped naked, and 'put in the bog.'"

became Earl of Tyrconnel; and it was conditioned that in future English sheriffs were to frame panels and English judges to expound the law throughout Ulster, and the chiefs were to hold their land directly from the Crown. There was great rage among the soldiers and officials of Dublin that there were no lands to be distributed after all. But there were better things in store for them than they thought of.

The substitution of a feudal tenure for the native *gavelkinde* (the tenure of the not utterly barbarous county of Kent to this day) had long been a main object with English statesmen. Henry had striven hard for it. He desired, according to the eminent historian whom I have already quoted,* "to change the loose order of inheritance for an orderly succession," and to confer upon the chiefs "a legitimate jurisdiction derived from the king"—for it was the interest of the chiefs, it seems, the bountiful prince had in view, but while they had arms in their hands, there was no persuading the perverse Celts to accept this royal benevolence; now however the reform was duly accomplished. Under the Celtic tenure a chief was only joint owner with the clan; by this change he became in the eye of the English law absolute proprietor of the soil. It was a boon like

---

* Mr. Froude's *The English in Ireland.*

that which Satan in popular fable bestows on his dupes. When the chief possessed only a life interest, he could forfeit in case of attainder only a life interest; when he became proprietor in fee, he would forfeit the estate; and in good time, as we shall see, three-fourths of the soil of Ireland was confiscated to the Crown under the operation of this royal bounty. With the sept it fared still worse than with the chief; at one stroke from joint owners of the tribal lands they were reduced to the condition of tenants at will, and deprived of an inheritance to which their title was as good in the court of conscience as Elizabeth's to the throne of Henry. And tenants at will, for the most part, they remain to this day.

Before quitting the reign of this queen it will be instructive to reiterate, that her agents, not merely in the cases cited, but habitually, practised arts which we are taught to attribute only to Italian nobles and Eastern despots. To cut off dangerous chiefs some were trapped by proffers of friendship and made prisoners for life, some were poisoned with gifts of choice food sent to them with profuse pledges of friendship; others were slaughtered on their own hearths in the exercise of hospitality to their assassins, and many were inveigled to public conferences that they might be more conveniently murdered in batches. Not the Irish annals alone, but the State Papers of the period supply conclusive evidence of this system, and of the official authority under which it was practised. It helped, doubtless, to stamp on the native mind an ideal of Sassenach duplicity which Englishmen find revolting and incredible.*

While the submission of O'Neill was being completed James I. came to the throne. There was great joy in Ireland at the accession of the young King of Scots, for while he was still a pretender he had assiduously cultivated the good-will of the Irish, as a prince of their own Milesian stock, and the son of a queen who was reputed to have died a martyr for the Catholic faith.† Now, it might be hoped, the nation would have fair play at least, and even perhaps a gleam of court favour. But his English coun-

---

* One notable and characteristic instance must be specified. In Hugh O'Neill's war Hugh O'Donnell went to Spain to solicit speedy help, but the weapon which Shane O'Neill narrowly escaped, awaited him on the foreign shore, and was more skilfully tempered this time. He died by poison administered by an agent employed by the Irish Executive for the purpose; and Carew announced the joyful news to Lord Mountjoy, the commander-in-chief, with an enthusiasm somewhat mitigated by shame. (Calendar of State Papers, 1602.) But Mr. Froude is not ashamed; his excuse for the poisoning of Irishmen under Elizabeth would justify the same policy under Queen Victoria. Speaking of one of these assassinations, he says, "In the desperation of such scenes as were witnessed daily in an Irish rebellion, any means seems lawful which may help to end them."

† Hugh Reilly, Irish Chancellor to James II. at St. Germains, avers (in his History of Ireland), that James I. sent supplies to Hugh O'Neill during his war against Elizabeth.

sellors knew that he could scarce hold the English throne if he made concessions to Ireland, and one of his earliest acts was a proclamation announcing that liberty of conscience he could not grant. But though religious liberty must be refused, English law would be introduced to every part of the island, the sword be sheathed, and every man indiscriminately taken into the favour of the king's majestie.* In this happy era the Irish were destined to learn how much more destructive an instrument than the sword that was sheathed is the inkhorn, when it is placed on the council-board to frame Acts of Parliament and Orders in Council. Though gallant adventurers could no longer, in the language of the *Pacata Hibernia*, "have the killing of some Irish" as a morning's pastime, they might still, if they were skilful, enjoy much the same recreation, in the way of devising beneficial measures for the country.

In the transactions now to be briefly described, and which form the foundations of our modern history, English writers in general are agreed that the paramount nation exhibited singular wisdom and benevolence. Through constantly changing and troubled times they were always right; right when they did in Ireland the

---

. * Sir John Davies. It was at the opening of this new era that Sir John, then Attorney-General, made the conclusive admission regarding the previous government of the country, quoted at page 32.

exact reverse of what they were accustomed to do at home; right, by a singular good fortune, when they set aside rules of morality and justice, which elsewhere are of permanent authority.

Lord Bacon, with whom ideas grew plentifully, had a suggestion at the service of the new king as profitable as the "princelie policie" which he taught his predecessor. He was of opinion that a great settlement of English husbandmen in Ireland able to guard as well as to till the land, would help to secure the interest of the Crown. Till this was done Ireland was not effectually reduced, as Sir Edward Coke afterwards declared, "for there was ever a back-door in the north." The only question was where to plant them. O'Neill and Tyrconnell had proved dangerous adversaries; they possessed a fertile territory, and as their "loose order of inheritance" had been duly changed into "an orderly succession," they were quite ripe for confiscation. But they had been ostentatiously received into favour at the close of the late war, and some decent pretence for destroying them so soon was indispensable. It was found in a letter conveniently dropped in the precincts of Dublin Castle, disclosing a new conspiracy. Of a conspiracy there was not then, and has not been since discovered, any evidence worth recording. The letter was probably forged according to the practise of the times; but where

so noble a booty was to be distributed by the Crown, one can conceive how ill-timed and disloyal any doubt of their treason would have appeared at the Court of James, or of the Lord Deputy. They were proclaimed traitors, and fled to the Continent to solicit aid from the Catholic Powers.*
Without delay James and his counsellors set to work. The King applied to the City of London to take up the

---

* In his "Flight of the Earls" the Rev. C. P. Meehan has painted with singular power and feeling the adventures of O'Neill and his associates at foreign courts, beseeching help in vain; till at length tired of the hopeless task one after another laid down his weary head in a foreign grave. It may be noted that the precise offence imputed to the chiefs, to justify an enormous confiscation, was soliciting aid against their lawful sovereign from Philip of Spain. James, who considered this offence worthy of so signal a punishment, received agents in his own Court from the Netherlands, soliciting his aid against the same Philip, who was the lawful sovereign of Flanders and Brabant quite as much as James was lawful sovereign of Tyrone and Tyrconnel. But one learns from a study of Anglo-Irish history to discriminate. When a Catholic nation invites the assistance of a Catholic prince, they are perverse rebels properly punished with the heaviest penalties; but when a Protestant nation invites the assistance of a Protestant prince, they are generous patriots vindicating the rights of conscience and of their native country. English historians still speak of Tyrone's new treason. His cotemporary, Sir John Davies, took a different view of the transaction. "As for us, that are here (in Ireland) we are glad to see the day wherein the countenance and majesty of the law and civil government hath *banished* Tyrone out of Ireland, which the best army in Europe, and the expense of two million of sterling pounds had not been able to bring to pass."— Letter of Sir John Davies, quoted in Moore's *History of Ireland*. Vol. IV.

lands of the wild Irish. They were well watered, he assured them, plentifully supplied with fuel, with good store of all the necessaries for man's sustenance; and moreover yielded timber, hides, tallow, canvas, and cordage for the purposes of commerce. The Companies of Skinners, Fishmongers, Haberdashers, Vintners and the like thereupon became Absentee Proprietors and have guzzled Irish rents in city feasts and holiday excursions to Ireland from that day to this. Six counties in Ulster were confiscated, and not merely the chiefs, but the entire population dispossessed. The fruitful plains of Armagh, the deep pastoral glens that lie between the sheltering hills of Donegal, the undulating meadow lands stretching by the noble lakes and rivers of Fermanagh, passed from the race which had possessed them since before the redemption of mankind. It is not difficult to see in imagination the old race, broken by battle and suffering, and deprived, by a trick of state, of their hereditary chiefs, retiring slowly and with bitter hearts before the stranger. The alluvial lands were given to English courtiers whom the Scotch king found it necessary to placate, and to Scotch partisans whom he dared not reward in England. The peasants driven out of the tribal lands to burrow in the hills or bogs were not treated according to any law known among civilised men. Under Celtic tenure the treason of the chief, if he committed treason, affected them no more than the offences of a tenant for life affect a remainder man in our modern practice. Under the feudal system they were innocent feudatories who would pass with the forfeited land to the Crown, with all their personal rights undisturbed.

The method of settlement is stated with commendable simplicity by the latest historian. The "plantators" got all the land worth their having; what was not worth their having—the barren mountains and trackless morass, which after two centuries still in many cases yield no human food—were left to those who in the language of an Act of Parliament of the period were "natives of the realm of Irish blood, being descended from those who did inherit and possess the land." Lest the frugality of the Celts should enable them to peacefully regain some of their possessions, it was strictly conditioned that no plantator or servitor should alienate his portion, or any part thereof, to the mere Irish. The confiscated territory amounted to two millions of acres. "Of these a million and a half," says Mr. Froude, "bog, forest, and mountain were restored to the Irish. The half million acres of fertile land were settled with families of Scottish and English Protestants."*

---

* I have taken Mr. Froude's computation for the sake of not overstating the case; but the Rev. George Hill, a Presbyterian clergyman, who has written a more careful and conscientious history of these transactions, states the result differently. The confiscation (which consisted

It was in this manner that the famous Plantation of Ulster was founded. The natives were discontented with these arrangements, and their perversity has been visited with eloquent censure by indignant critics down to our own day. There is reason to believe, however, that if a settlement of Irish Catholics had been made in England by Mary or James II., on whom the best lands of Norfolk and Suffolk, Essex and Sussex, Kent and Surrey, were bestowed, while the English were left only the forest, mountain, and morass, that that just and temperate people would not have entirely approved of the transaction, and might even be tempted to call it in question when an opportunity offered.

The new comers have been painted in unfavourable colours by critics not unfriendly to the plantation. In many cases it is probable they were good soldiers or skilful husbandmen, who under more favourable conditions would have been an element of strength to the country. But the settlement had the fever of usurpation upon it.

---

of the entire counties of Armagh, Tyrone, Coleraine, Donegal, Fermanagh and Cavan), covered about four million acres; and according to Mr. Hill, the native landlords and tenants were all, with one or two exceptions, displaced and dispossessed; the native gentry getting shreds of freehold in the most barren districts of each of the six counties, and the native tenants being permitted to hold small patches under the English servitors (or military officers), and the English bishops who got share of the plunder. The counties of Down, Antrim, and Monaghan had been previously confiscated, and were not included in this Plantation.

The rightful owners were forthcoming, and the planters held by no higher title than naked force; good as long as force was on their side, but no longer. Fences were erected, fruit-trees planted, simple churches built, and after a time white-walled bawns rose in the midst of waving corn-fields and rosy orchards.* It was a pleasant sight to see; but within a gunshot of the gay harvest and garden, the remnant of the native race, to whom the land had descended since the Redemption, were pining in misery and bitter discontent. The barren hills or frozen bogs to which they were banished yielded little food except the milk of their kine.† "The mountainy men," so the new settlers contemptuously named them, would have been more magnanimous than any race who have lived on this globe, if they acquiesced patiently in the transfer. They could not forget, any more than their kinsmen in the Scottish Highlands, that

"The fertile plain, the softened vale
Were once the birthright of the Gael."

---

* "Bawn," a strong mansion with a fortified court yard.

† Some had no choice but to wander abroad like the victims of a modern extermination, for the mountain and morass could not provide for all. One hears later in Irish affairs of certain northern disturbers— "Creaghts, a race of barbarous rovers (says Leland) without any settled residence, wandering with their cattle in search of subsistence, to the great annoyance of the district which they visited," upon whom history has no mercy. What justification had they, indeed, for being without a home, to the inconvenience of quiet people provided with that asylum?

, If their efforts to "spoil the spoiler," and "from the robber rend his prey,"* do not thrill sympathetic boudoirs, and if the scenes of their exploits are not the annual haunt of sentimental tourists, it is not because the exploits were different from those so favoured, but because a Walter Scott has not yet arisen to interpret them to mankind.†

To obtain the sanction of the Irish Parliament, composed of feudatories of the Crown, to the practice of transferring property from hereditary owners to foreign protégés of the reigning sovereign, would have been difficult under any circumstances. But it was peculiarly difficult when the two races had just been declared equal in the eyes of the law, and some of the native chiefs sat with the old English and new English, and possessed an undoubted right to confirm or reject the royal scheme. But James was shown a device for evading the difficulty, exactly adapted to the temper of his mind, which he joyfully adopted. Forty

---

* *Lady of the Lake.*

† Such a poet may perhaps appear in unexpected places; for the Irish struggle has exercised a strange fascination over young imaginative Englishmen. Lord Macaulay began his splendid experiment in ballad poetry by singing the Celtic resistance to the invasion of Strongbow, Lord Lytton's first published poem, "O'Neill," had for its hero that unconquerable Hugh who so long baffled the arms of Elizabeth; and Southey has celebrated with passionate sympathy Robert Emmet, an Irish rebel who gave his life for his cause.

boroughs were created in a single day, consisting for the most part of townships, where towns were projected but not built, or of groups of three or four houses inhabited by a dozen or so of new settlers, to whom in some cases a charter had not yet been issued. These boroughs were authorised to select two members each, and when the new Parliament met, two hundred thousand English and Anglo-Irish of the religion of the Court were found to have more representatives than six times as many of the natives. The members for the new borough, were not likely to be troublesome to the Crown; they were chosen from the Lord Deputy's servants, attorneys' clerks, bankrupts, outlaws, and other persons in a servile or dependent condition. The authentic representatives of the people sent agents to James to complain of this abuse of the royal prerogative by which they were swamped in their own Parliament by the intrusion of nearly eighty unauthorised persons. James returned an answer, which the reader may consider inadequate, but which would certainly have seemed sufficient to any Stuart that ever reigned in England. Too many members? "The more the merrier," quoth he, "the fewer the better cheer."

But Sir John Davies, Speaker of the new Parliament was more politic than the king, and may indeed be regarded as the very high priest of plausibility in that day. He knew that the name and form of freedom had been granted to the nation, and clearly perceived that the form ought to be respected, though the substance might be skilfully filched away—a method of reforming Irish abuses which has never been permitted to fall into disuse. Under his direction the House of Commons admitted the wrong, and evaded the remedy. It was true that many members were "unduly elected," some (as the resolution recited) for "being judges, some for not being estated in their boroughs, some for being outlawed, excommunicated, and lastly, for being returned for places whose charters were not valid." It would greatly prejudice the public business, however, to create a delay just then; therefore the returns should not be questioned, but this resolution must, of course, not be drawn into a precedent. The native members withdrew in a rage, and the representatives of boroughs "whose charters were not valid," the bankrupt, outlawed, and excommunicated nominees of the Castle, declared the territory of O'Neill and O'Donnell forfeited to the Crown. Such a Parliament could scarcely be improved upon, and when leisure came the fraudulent boroughs were not called in question. They were never called in question, indeed, but carefully maintained by successive sovereigns and governments as a means of keeping Parliament in order, and, in the end, they contributed effectually to its destruction in the first memorable year of this century.

From this time forth the native race in the North have

had to maintain a ceaseless struggle for existence against a barren soil, a hostile government, and stern landlords resident in London, or blacker stranger living among them. The rent paid to the native chief was equivalent to a tax paid to the king; it was a return for services performed by the leader and representative of the people. The rent paid to his successor was paid for no equivalent or service whatever.*

The abolition of the loose method of inheritance (by which Irish lands used to pass to the right owners) was followed by another amelioration, without which it would have been incomplete. When a Catholic proprietor died leaving children under age, the king like a true father of his people undertook the charge of the orphans. The powers and functions of the Court of Wards founded by Henry VIII. were enlarged; and as James could not get a wife out of Spain for his son, on which condition he was

---

* In 1843, an investigation was made into the accounts of the Irish Society, which conducted the interest of the London Companies in Ulster. It appeared that in twenty-three years upwards of £100,000 had been spent on management; management being made to include more than £6,000 for tavern expenses, £5,000 for deputations who made little tours in Ireland, nearly £10,000 in fees distributed among the members themselves, and upwards of £20,000 in salaries, gratuities, donations, and incidental expenses incurred *in England*. It is nearly time that the arrangement which gives the fertile lands of Derry and Tyrone to Cockney tradesmen should be reconsidered.

ready to "kiss the Pope's pantoufle," he became an ardent Reformer, and it was ordered that the children should be strictly educated in the Reformed religion. If they were girls they were provided with Protestant husbands by James or Buckingham. This device proved a most successful stroke of State policy, and with the favours and blandishments of the Court judiciously distributed, did more than the laws of Henry and Elizabeth to win over the old families. Education is stronger than natural instincts or inherited opinions. The Janissaries were Christian orphans trained to be Mussulmen by the Sultan, and the most remorseless enemies of the Celt in the next generation were O'Briens and Butlers, who became more English than the English themselves.

In process of time the O'Brien became Earl of Thomond, the O'Healy, Earl of Donoghmore, the O'Quin, Earl of Dunraven, the O'Callaghan, Lord Lismore, the O'Neill, Lord O'Neill, and so forth; all partisans of the English interest, and the Established Church. The Anglo-Norman families went the same way; the Fitzgeralds, the Butlers, the De Courceys, the De Burgos, and the rest, made their submission to the State and the Church. From this time forth there were Irish courtiers in London. The chief, who lived among his people, and was a visible Providence, began to be replaced by an English cavalier who spent the revenue of the O'Brien's country, or the MacWilliams's country, in playing hazard with Buckingham, or junketting with the ladies of Whitehall.

The Catholics made strenuous appeals to the king for religious liberty, but with small success. Sir Walter Scott has left a picture of the pedantic folly of James in Romance* more vivid than any to be found in History; but it might receive some heightening touches from his Irish achievements. To a deputation of Irish Catholics who came to solicit liberty of conscience he said, " I take God to witness that if, after diligent study and conversations with learned men, I came to the conclusion that this Pope and his predecessors had been delegated by our Lord, I would stab any king (were I a subject), who would impugn their authority." That the Pope was delegated by our Lord, being exactly the belief of the applicants before him, a very awkward inference followed from this royal declaration.

The experiment in Ulster naturally provoked imitation. Charles I. was as eager to plant as his father. He was represented in Ireland by a trenchant Lord Deputy, remembered in that country as "Black Tom," and memorable in English history as Thomas Wentworth, Earl of Strafford. Wentworth resolved to make a settlement in Connaught to rival the settlement in Ulster. The first business was to clear out the owners in possession. The

---

* Fortunes of Nigel.

wildest inventions in "Candide," intended to illustrate human absurdity and wickedness, will not match the pretence on which the forfeiture of these estates was founded. In the previous reign when the king substituted "an orderly succession" for the Celtic method, the Connaught proprietors had duly submitted and paid him a heavy fine to have their new patents enrolled in Chancery. The officers of the Court, wilfully or ignorantly, omitted to make the proper entries in their books; and this misfeasance was declared by Court lawyers to have forfeited the lands of the province to the king. It is a maxim that no man can profit by his own fraud; but maxims are not made to bind sovereign princes. As the blessing of English law, however, had been extended to the whole nation, it was necessary that this opinion should be confirmed by the judgment of a Court and the verdict of a jury. If a dozen of his fellow-countrymen found a Connaught proprietor's title bad, calumny itself must be mute. Wentworth marched to the West at the head of a formidable military force, as "good lookers-on," he said, and accompanied by the necessary retinue of judges and lawyers to perform the judicial ceremony. Some of the juries were frightened into verdicts; some were wheedled into them, for to sharpen the persuasive power of the judges Wentworth secretly gave these learned personages a percentage on the forfeitures. But in Galway the juries were of opinion that, notwithstanding the misconduct of the officers of Chancery, the land did not belong to the king, but to the owners, and they found accordingly. Wentworth's method of encountering this difficulty may help to mitigate our surprise that the Irish people did not cordially love a system of jurisprudence, which undoubtedly secured equal justice to many generations of Englishmen. The jurors who found a verdict according to their conscience, and not according to the wishes of the Lord Deputy, were immediately brought before the Castle Chamber in Dublin, and fined £4,000 each and their estates seized till the fine was paid; a penalty the equivalent of which would impoverish many a noble of the present day. They were further required to acknowledge their offence in public court on bended knees. The lawyers who had the wickedness to plead for the native proprietors were tendered the Oath of Supremacy, which as Catholics they could not take; and declining to take it were excluded from future practise. The sheriff who summoned the jurors was dealt with in a more decisive fashion: he was first fined and then flung into prison, where he was kept till he died of the process; an example to future officials to array their panels more discreetly.

This was not Strafford's only experiment in manipulating juries. The London Parliament on the occasion of his impeachment, cited among the catalogue of his offences in

Ireland—"that jurors who gave their verdict according to their consciences, were censured in the Castle Chamber in great fines; sometimes pilloried, with loss of ears, and bored through the tongue, and sometimes marked in the forehead, with other infamous punishments." Strafford, who was a wise tyrant, did other work however. He got flaxseed from Holland, and workmen from Belgium, and fostered a linen trade among the plantators, which is prosperous to this day. Fortunately for Ulster linen was not a staple of England.

Strafford's most notable proceeding is still to be mentioned. Though Charles's character as a compound of egotism and faithlessness is one of the most familiar studies in English history, it may borrow a characteristic touch from Irish records. Before these transactions he appealed in sore stress to his Irish subjects for a grant of money; the Catholics took his wants into consideration and offered a subsidy of £120,000—an enormous sum in that day—provided that no proprietor sixty years in undisturbed possession should be troubled respecting his title; and that Catholics should be allowed to practise as barristers without taking the oath of supremacy. Charles took the money, and promised the "Graces" (so they were named) which they desired. The Puritans however grew daily stronger, and to keep the promise of tolerating Papists, even in so small a matter as not cheating them out of their estates, soon became inconvenient. Some of the bishops of the Irish Establishment transmitted a fierce remonstrance to England against any concession to Catholics, and as Charles was a good Churchman and loved his bishops, he was sorely perplexed; but above all there was the glory and profit of making a plantation in Connaught no longer possible if he kept his word.* Wentworth saw

---

* The protest of the Bishops drawn up by Archbishop Ussher, one of the ablest men the Irish Establishment has produced, is commended to the attention of persons who are accustomed to clamour about the bigotry of Rome. "The Religion of the Papists is Superstitious and Idolatrous, "their Faith and Doctrines erroneous and heretical, their Church, in "respect of both, Apostatical: to give them, therefore, a *Toleration*, or "to consent that they may, freely, exercise their Religion, and profess "their Faith and Doctrine, is a grievous sin."

The principle which lay at the root of this persecuting spirit is curious. The Puritans insisted upon the right of private judgment. They were fighting for religious freedom against a persecuting king. Independants, Anabaptists, and Brownists were not to be disturbed in their liberty of conscience. To set up a new creed in a new conventicle was lawful. But if a man's private judgment led him to prefer the faith that prevailed throughout the bulk of Christendom, then the rule did not apply.

Lord Macaulay, who seems always to have proceeded upon the assumption that justice is a luxury, like Bass's beer and Holloway's ointment, intended specially for British enjoyment, says of this era, "One part of the empire was so unhappily circumstanced that, at that time, its misery was necessary to our happiness, and its slavery to our freedom."* . This maxim describes the policy to which he was himself a party in the reign of Queen Victoria as accurately as Cromwell's in the Commonwealth ; and to my thinking, is as base a rule of conduct as any that can be picked out of Macchiavelli.

* In the *Edinburgh Review* article "Milton."

an easy way out of the difficulty; let him simply not keep his word; and he, for his part, was willing to assist so worthy a purpose by bearing all the blame. Charles's whole character is painted in the two facts, that he broke his promise without scruple, after he had spent the subsidy, and thankfully accepted Strafford's offer to stand between him and the infamy he had incurred. He even improved in time on the teaching of his minister. Later, when the Puritans determined to destroy Strafford himself, the king passionately assured him that not a hair of his head would he suffer to be touched; but when he discovered that it would be dangerous to keep his word, he graciously pronounced the ceremonial "Le roi le veut" over the Act of Parliament which sent him to the block; a transaction in which the student will probably recognise what is called poetic justice.

Nearly a generation had elapsed since the Plantation of Ulster, when the troubles between Charles and his Parliament began. The middle classes and many of the gentry distrusted his policy in Church and State, and feared his leanings towards Rome. They had some ground for their fears. His wife was a devout Catholic; his chief adviser in spiritual affairs, Archbishop Laud, was a High Churchman, to whom a Catholic was more acceptable than a Sectary; and to Charles himself, Rome was not so odious as Geneva. By this time a great change had come over the English people. They had grown graver and more thoughtful than at the era of the Reformation. As soon as the stern authority of Henry was removed, a sect sprang up which aimed to model the new Church on the doctrine and system of Calvin. From the strictness of their tenets, and the severity of their practices, they were named, partly in ridicule, the Puritans. These men were more in earnest than the courtly ecclesiastics, and more intelligible to the people, and their opinions spread rapidly, chiefly among the industrious class, as Wesleyan Methodism spread in a later age, for the same reason. They had embarrassed James by questions of prerogative, and they set up a fierce parliamentary opposition as often as want of money compelled Charles to summon a parliament. John Pym, John Hampden, and other men of remarkable ability, led this party, and it soon became plain that the issue would be civil war. The Puritans were undoubtedly contending for liberty, but it was liberty in which Prelatists and Papists should have no share. Their success has been a blessing to mankind; but it is a blessing because mankind have peremptorily rejected many of the opinions which distinguished the Puritans from the rest of the nation.

Secretly instigated by the Parliamentary leaders, the Scots rose against the king and invaded England in considerable force, and Charles summoned to his aid the army which Wentworth maintained in Ireland; an army recruited in part from Irish Catholics. In the House of Commons this project evoked a storm of resistance It was permissible to call a Scottish army into England, and it was a natural right, which no one would be mad enough to dispute, to send an English army into Ireland, but if an Irish army were brought into England, on any pretence whatever, that was an outrage sufficient to release subjects from their allegiance. The Irish, who did not quite see the force of this distinction, began to bestir themselves. They heard of threats in London that Popery must be extirpated; Pym, in the House of Commons, boasted, it was said, that Parliament would not leave a Papist in Ireland; they noted the successful rebellion of the Scots, they saw their old enemies in conflict, and the time seemed propitious to regain their ancient lands, and to save such as remained from bribed judges and panic-stricken juries. Roger O'Moore, a man greatly gifted both to project and to persuade, and whom contemporaries of all parties pronounce of unblemished honour, brought leading men together, kindled them with his own convictions, and in a short time there was a genuine conspiracy on foot to seize the seat of government, and summon the Irish race to arms. For now again there had arisen among the Irish a Statesman; one who not only recognised injustice and pitied it, of which sort there was no scarcity, but who saw how to amend or end it.

Owen Connolly, servant of one of the conspirators, betrayed his master, several of the leaders were seized, and the government in Dublin put effectually on their guard. But the North was beyond their control. There the clans who had been pillaged by James, or their immediate descendants, rose on an autumn night forty thousand strong, led by Sir Phelim (still remembered by Ulster peasants as Phelemy) O'Neill and other chiefs of their own blood, drove out the English and Scotch settlers, and repossessed themselves of their ancient tribal lands. This is the transaction known to English writers as the "Great Popish Rebellion," and the "Popish Massacre;" the leader of the rising being a man educated by the Court of Wards as a Protestant. By whatever contumelious nickname it may be branded, what happened in Ireland is what would have happened in any branch of the human family. When a favourable opportunity offered they "spoiled the spoiler." So the Saxons dealt with their Norman conquerors, as far as their power and opportunity permitted, and the Dutch with their Spanish conquerors, and the Sicilians with their French conquerors.* Though there were dreadful excesses

---

* While this volume is passing through the press, the Italians are celebrating the six hundredth anniversary of the Sicilian Vespers; of which the Rising in Ulster was but a pale copy. Had the Sicilians failed, what a scarecrow John of Procida would have made in French history?

committed by both parties in the end, it is certain beyond all controversy, that the first aim of the Irish was to regain their own without any sacrifice of life. On the night of the rising, and during the six days that followed, only one man was killed; a fact which stamps with complete certainty their original purpose.* When blood is shed it

---

* Lord Chichester wrote to the King, "they took four considerable towns and have slain only one man."

The evidence for the original intentions of the insurgents is to be found in the proclamations which they issued, in the correspondence of the Lords Deputy with the Parliament, and in all moderately fair historians of the period. Two short extracts from writers, both of whom were Protestant clergymen, and one an Englishman, will suffice.

"It was resolved" [by the Irish party] "not to kill any, but where, of necessity, they should be forced thereunto by opposition."—Warner's *History of the Rebellion.*

"In the beginning of the insurrection it was determined" [by the Irish] "that the enterprise should be conducted in every quarter with as little bloodshed as possible."—Leland's *History of Ireland.*

Mr. Carlyle, the sternest critic of the era among writers not wilfully unfair, is compelled to admit that the original Rising was justifiable. "Their cause we can all now see was just," he says in his "Cromwell." The original justice of the cause sufficiently covers, in his eyes, the excesses of the French Revolution, but is not permitted even to palliate inevitable gusts of revenge and retaliation in what was substantially a peasant insurrection. In truth he never took the pains to understand this era in Ireland. The most equivocal sentence that can be found in his historical writings, it seems to me, is the admission that he wrote of it with wholly inadequate knowledge. "The history of it does not form itself," he declares, "into a picture, but remains only a huge blot—an indiscriminate blackness, which the human memory cannot willingly charge itself with!" Not so; on the contrary, to those who have studied

is like kindling the prairie; no one can any longer pretend to limit the devastation. But there were some signal instances of moderation; certain priests it is recorded concealed fugitives under their altars;* and Dr. Bedell, a bishop of the Protestant Establishment, who had distinguished himself by humane conduct in his day of power, was permitted in the very focus of the insurrection, to fill his house with English settlers, and shelter them from all molestation.

The contemporary accounts of the transaction are

---

the period, the Norman Conquest, or the first War of the Roses, does not form a more picturesque and consecutive panorama than the confiscation of Ulster, the rising of the plundered population, and the merciless measures taken by the English parliament to perpetuate the original robbery. To get at the truth, it is true, was not easy, for books containing the case of the Irish were few and inaccessible. It was more than half a century after the Rising before even a modified defence of it could get a hearing in England, or was permissible in Ireland. To deny the wildest fables of the Puritans, during that time, was to be charged with desiring to revive the massacre on the first favourable opportunity; and behind these impediments, in Mr. Carlyle's case, lay the inherent difficulty that this man of genius, who commonly saw deep into the motive power of transactions, never on this question. outgrew the original prejudices of a Scotch Covenanter.

* Leland's *History of Ireland*. Leland (it is necessary to keep clearly in mind) was a Professor of Trinity College, Dublin, and a Chaplain to the Lord-Lieutenant in the time of George III. The Scotch were treated with peculiar forbearance. The Irish made proclamation, on pain of death, that no Scotsman should be molested in body, goods, or lands.—Carte's *Ormond*, i., 178.

quite as untrustworthy as the narratives of Dangerfield
and his confederates. The settlers depended absolutely
on the support of England for maintaining their position. Many of them had suffered grievously, and the
remainder were in danger of losing the fruit of all their
toil and enterprise. What sort of stories they sent to
Westminster under such circumstances, to inflame the zeal
of their partizans, may be conceived. All Puritan England was ready to believe, and eager to hear, new marvels
of Irish iniquity. Pious tears and rage were excited by a
description of the ghosts of murdered Protestants appearing
in broad daylight, day after day, on the bridge of Portadown, wringing their hands and uttering piercing shrieks
for an avenger. One peculiarly stubborn ghost held his
ground for more than a month. A bishop was among the
witnesses of these impressive facts; which exhibited, as
one can conceive, heaven itself among the allies of the
plantators.*

The broad sheets published in London from day to day,
by the Parliament and its partisans, were as shameless as
the inventions of a Hindoo against a fallen enemy. But

---

* There is in Trinity College, Dublin, a mass of depositions intended
to establish these astonishing phenomena, and others nearly as marvellous. Edmund Burke, who personally examined the documents, speaks
of the "rascally collection in the College, relative to the pretended
massacre of 1641. Mr. Froude of course accepts this "rascally collection"
as if they were so many proofs of Holy Writ

they did their work. They fed the prejudice of the English people against the "Queen's Party," and to this hour they are the familiar materials of English History. The best of them is abundantly leavened with falsehood, but some of them must have been invented in London, for no plantator would have ventured on fabrications so glaring and palpable. Among the great leaders of the rebels for example, we find the illustrious potentates, Lords Matquers, Dulon, Don Lace, Cargena, Limbrey, and Lewricole. These great unknown or their followers, committed excesses in districts of commensurate obscurity. They burned Lognall, and Toyhull; seized upon fifteen towns in the great county of Monno (by some read Conno), laid seige to Anney, and committed unheard of cruelties in the populous and Protestant county of Warthedeflowr. In some of them Dublin is seized by the natives, in others O'Neill is a prisoner in the hands of the Irish Government. One Tract contains a circumstantial account by "One of God's ministers" of a new gunpowder plot, to blow up the flourishing town of Rockoll, six miles from Dublin, while the king's army were in the act of passing through it; but fortunately this atrocity was prevented by the gallant conduct of a gentleman to whom posterity has been singularly ungrateful, Mr. Carot Topey.*

---

* See Thorpe's Tracts, a collection of contemporary brochures, in the Royal Irish Academy, Dublin, collected and presented by Mr. Thorpe.

The theory finally adopted by English and Anglo-Irish writers generally, with respect to this transaction, when the clouds of prejudice and misrepresentation had blown away, is perplexing to human reason. To seize the hereditary lands of the Irish race, and drive out the inhabitants from the pastoral valleys and alluvial plains which they and theirs had enjoyed since the dawn of history, was a wise stroke of statesmanship it seems; but to seize the same lands occupied for a single generation by English settlers, and drive out the inhabitants, in order to replace the original population in their own possessions, was a crime of incredible greed and cruelty. A title founded on the naked ground of conquest is for ever liable to the right of resumption or reconquest, which establishes a similar title in some other persons. Six years earlier the Scotch had risen in defence of their religion, and for the redress of civil grievances. And they succeeded. No person has yet suggested an intelligible reason why the Irish also should not defend their religion, and procure the redress of grievances? In modern times, when the original history of the massacre is well understood to have been partly a scare, partly a lie, the chief complaint against the Irish is that they laid waste a flourishing settlement where goodly men were enjoying the fruits of their industry in holy peace. But the contemporary evidence is of a different character. The last glimpse we catch of the

Scotch plantators exhibits them enduring, from English Bishops and nobles, the same stripes which Dundee and Dalzell inflicted on Cameronians and Covenanters a generation later—reduced to such a plight indeed that there would seem but little left for the Irish enemy to do. In a petition to the English Commons in 1640, the Presbyterians of Antrim, Down, and Tyrone, declare that by "the cruelties, severities, and arbitrarie proceedings of civil magistrates, but principally through the sway of the prelacy with their faction, our souls are starved, our estates undone, our families empoverished, and many lives among us cut off and destroyed." They summed up the result. "Our cruel taskmasters have made us, who were once a people, to become, as it were, no people, an astonishment to ourselves, the object of pittie and amazement to others."*

The array of authorities for the common English view of the rising is very imposing, having the august name of John Milton at its head. But it is not more certain that Titus Oates' story of the Popish Plot was a fabrication, than that John Milton's specific statements about the Irish rebellion were unfounded and impossible. He placed the number of the massacred at 610,000. The Protestant population of the island, including soldiers in garrison and officials in Dublin, and the great towns, amounting at that time to little over

---

* Humble Petition of the Protestants, &c. Thorpe's Tracts.

200,000. Temple, who is the unrelenting enemy of the Irish, estimates the number in his History of the transaction, at 150,000; and Clarendon, the royalist Historian, reduces it to 50,000. These were guesses more or less wild. Cromwell issued a commission to investigate the wrongs endured by the British in Ireland, and Cromwell's commission, before which the maddest evidence was produced, and where the same incident is reported by various witnesses, and counted over and over, fixes the number of murders at 2,109, to which 1,900 cases, supposed to have occurred during the Confederate war, are added. If we accept as authentic the report of a fanatical commission, before whom no evidence on the part of the Irish was heard, and who believed in ghosts shrieking in the broad day for a Protestant avenger, Milton multiplied every murder by more than a hundred!* Fairly judged at this day, it must

---

*Milton, it must be admitted with shame, is no better than a party pamphleteer in this business, who defends a bad cause, badly. The English used their title to Ireland, he declared "with tenderness and moderation;" and he bases the title, (the legitimacy of which of course admits of no doubt) on the ground of piracies committed by the natives before the Norman Conquest! From which one may deduce the amazing doctrine, on the authority of a great moralist, that the Normans, having seized upon England by a prodigious stroke of piracy, became entitled to punish a neighbouring nation on the ground that their ancestors had anticipated this offence by committing piracy, on a diminutive scale, several generations earlier! His method of dealing with the imputed massacre is still worse. Of the 200,000 Protestants, 120,000 were in Ulster. A large proportion were in garrison or in walled towns which did not fall into the hands of the Irish, many took shelter in Derry and

be admitted that the transfer of the land back to its
original owners was made with as little premeditated
violence as in any agrarian revolution with which it can be
fairly brought into comparison. Bloody reprisals were the
custom of the age. In the Netherlands, in Italy, and in
France, the faction of the Catholics and the faction of the
Reformers killed and ravaged without remorse. That a
race whose chiefs had been trapped like wild beasts, or assassinated in the very offices of hospitality, among whom the
tragedy of the *Pacata Hibernia*, and the kindred tragedy
of the Plantation were performed, should have been stung
into no deadlier a humour will be for ever a marvel to men
who have studied human history and human nature. The
outrages shamefully exaggerated were no part of the
original design. The rising, when it fell under the guidance of Roger O'Moore, finally swelled into a revolution,
had its parliament at Kilkenny, to which Charles sent
ambassadors, and its armies in the field, to which in the

Coleraine, and a considerable number, it is admitted, were sent to
Dublin, in the first instance, under convoy, by the Irish leaders. In
Munster there were few Protestants, in Connaught scarcely any except
soldiers in garrison. Dealing with this state of facts, Milton, who, as
Latin Secretary to Cromwell, had the duty of presenting the case to
Europe, wrote in this strain:

"The rebellion and horrid massacre of the English Protestants in Ireland, to the amount of 154,000 in the province of Ulster only, by their
own computation; which, added to the other three, makes up the total
sum of that slaughter, in all likelihood, *four times as great*."

end, he would gladly have committed his cause, and conducted its measures with notable clemency and moderation.*

At the period of the Rising, the Lords Justices were Sir John Parsons and Sir John Borlase. Parsons, who was one of the greediest and most unscrupulous adventurers of whom history has left a record, was the leading spirit. He pursued with brutal frankness the policy which had secretly influenced the statesmen of the Pale at every critical era since the Invasion; he aimed to make peace impossible that forfeited estates might be plentiful. The Catholic peers and gentlemen of English descent had little national

---

* Unless on the hypothesis that there is a separate scheme of divine and human justice, and a separate law of nature, applicable to Ireland, it is difficult to account for the contradictory judgment which a man ordinarily so wise and just as Mr. Carlyle, applies to nearly indentical circumstances in Ireland and France. In Ireland the agricultural population driven wild by pillage and oppression, rose and repossessed themselves of lands recently taken from them, and in the process committed and endured cruel excesses: in France the agricultural population, also long oppressed and pillaged, rose and burned the châteaux of the noblesse, who had possessed them for centuries, killed the owners whenever they could find them, and when their partizans were in prison rose in conjunction with a city mob and murdered them in cold blood. Of the Irish transaction Mr. Carlyle has written a vehement and unmeasured condemnation. Of the French massacre he says "Horrible in lands that had known equal justice. Not so unnatural in lands that had never known it. *Le sang qui coule est il donc si pur?* asks Barnave, intimating that the gallows, though by irregular methods, had its own."—*Carlyle's French Revolution.*

spirit, and some of them were ready to prove their loyalty by taking up arms against the Northern Irish. But Parsons and his associates at the Privy Council determined to treat all Papists on the same footing. They were disarmed indescriminately. A few wished to retire to England, but permission was refused. They were ordered to reside on their estates, and not to return to Dublin on pain of death. That living at home might not be unduly agreeable, they were forbidden to retain the arms necessary for the defence of their houses against marauders. Some whom he chose to suspect, were put to the torture to extract a confession of their complicity with O'Neill. In short he left them no choice but to fight in self-defence, and at length they took up arms. Certain priests had distinguished themselves, as we have seen, in protecting the English fugitives in the North, and the Council checked this dangerous practice by ordering that all priests who fell into the hands of the army should be forthwith put to death. The English parliament highly approved of these measures, and solemnly resolved that no toleration should thenceforth be given to Popery in Ireland. To give full effect to their determination a loan was raised upon two millions and a half of "profitable lands," which it was agreed to take from the owners and sell to English adventurers.

In the Irish Parliament, called the Confederation of Kil-

kenny, the Catholics of both races were fully represented.
Don Eugenio O'Neill, known in Irish annals as Owen Roe,
a soldier who had acquired skill and experience in the
armies of Spain, came to the aid of his countrymen.
Throughout the war he exhibited sagacity, soldiership, and
patriotism, but he was constantly thwarted by the Anglo-
Irish, who were more solicitous for the security of Charles
than for the rights of the nation. It is the glory of
Hampden and Falkland to have loved England better than
they loved the king; and Owen Roe certainly loved Ireland better than he loved the king. The Confederation
established a regular government under the title of the
Supreme Council, got an army into the field in each of the
four provinces, coined money, sent agents to Rome and the
great Catholic powers, issued letters of marque to privateers, and established free trade with the Continent, from
which arms and amunition were obtained plentifully. It
was not the least of its achievements that it set up a
printing press, a machine so rare, and so restricted by law,
that there was but one at the seat of English government
in Dublin.

The war which this national government maintained was
distinguished by clemency and good faith. They were
apparently determined that the national cause, represented
by the leading men of the nation, should be clearly distinguishable from the rising of plundered peasants in the

North; and it will be so distinguished by fair critics for ever. When strong places fell into their hands they murdered no garrisons, sacked no cities, burned no churches, put no peaceful inhabitants to the sword, though these crimes were being committed against them at the moment. The English Parliament directed that all Irish Papists fighting for the King in Scotland (where the Catholics had sent Charles some aid), or at sea, should be denied quarter, and Irish soldiers were strung up in batches, and their wives and children flung into the sea in pursuance of this order. If the Catholics had retaliated who could be surprised; but the Supreme Council forbade retaliation. In the first year of the war the garrison of Drogheda received the submission of 1200 Protestants, who were admitted to terms and treated with humanity. And this was their common custom. They practised forbearance to lengths, which, in face of the provocation they endured, was admirable and wonderful. For the soldiers of the Parliament fought under the inspiration of men who declared that one Papist must not be left in Ireland. The most ferocious of these soldiers was Sir Charles Coote. His career is an unbroken record of murder and plunder. We read of garrisons put to the sword after they had laid down their arms, of towns, villages, and manor houses wantonly burned, of growing crops laid waste, of priests and friars knocked on the head whenever they were encountered, all told, as coolly as a modern reporter describes a battue; till at length a musket ball brought his achievements to a sudden end. Munroe, a Scotch soldier, rivalled Coote in barbarity; he is described as roasting fugitives—many hundred it is alleged—in a wood, which he fired to destroy them—laying waste the harvest and renewing the other horrors of the *Pacata Hibernia*, till happily he encountered Owen Roe, as we shall see. Lord Inchiquin, the head of a family which inherited the blood of Brian Borhoime, has left a blacker memory than Coote or Munroe. He is still execrated in Munster as Murrough of the Burnings. The achievement by which he is best remembered is the sacking of the ancient Church on the Rock of Cashel. He offered terms, it is said, to the garrison empowering them to depart with all the honours of war, but they refused to leave the priests and citizens at his mercy. A prodigious slaughter ensued; when the struggle was over nearly a thousand dead bodies of the besieged and the besiegers, (for the garrison fought gallantly) strewed the church and its approaches. Twenty priests were massacred, and one of their confreres has left this vivid picture of the scenes which ensued. "The altars were overturned; the images that were painted on wood were consigned to the flames; those on canvas were used as bedding for the horses, or were cut into sacks for burdens. The great crucifix which stood at the entrance of the choir, as if it had been guilty of treason, was beheaded, and soon after its hands and feet were amputated. With a like fury did they rage against all the other chapels of the city; gathering together the sacred vases and all the most precious vestments, they formed a procession in ridicule of our ceremonies. They marched through the public squares, wearing the sacred vestments, having the priests' caps on their heads, and inviting to Mass those whom they met on the way. A beautiful statue of the immaculate Virgin taken from our Church was borne along (the head being broken off) in mock state, with laughter and ridicule. The leader of the Puritan army had the temerity to assume the archiespiscopal mitre, and boast that he was now not only governor and lieutenant of Munster, but also Archbishop of Cashel."*

The Confederate Council ordered that "accurate accounts" of these outrages should be collected. Strict accuracy was scarcely to be expected under the circumstances; the accounts were afterwards published, and it may well be that they were exaggerated by rage and horror; but they rested, I do not doubt, on a substantial basis of truth. They can scarcely be matched, in human annals, for cold blooded and wanton cruelty. They record

---

* Narrative of the Irish Superior of the Jesuits, cited in the Right Reverend Dr. Moran's Historical Sketch of the Persecution of the Irish Catholics.

the burning of aged men and women, the murder of
the blind and disabled, of women who bore other
lives, and the drowning of batches of unarmed peasants
with their wives and little ones. Two hundred women
and children, they allege, were smothered in a cave
in Donegal; three hundred men, women, and children
who sought shelter in Derry were butchered by the
garrison; five hundred persons were arrested by soldiers at
Newry and flung in successive batches into the river; Irish
soldiers, who yielded on terms at Clongoweswood, were hung
as soon as they had submitted; and a hundred and fifty
women and children (camp followers it may be presumed),
slaughtered; three hundred peaceful farmers and farm
labourers with their families were murdered by the Parliamentarians quartered in Drogheda; eighty-eight inhabitants of Bandon were tied back to back and flung into the
river by the garrison, (the same garrison are described in
another of their slaughter houses as seizing young children
by the legs, and knocking their brains out against the
wall), a hundred and fifty persons of both sexes at Termonfechan were roasted to death by setting fire to a furze-cover
in which they had taken shelter. And so forth through a
long catalogue of cruelty and perfidy; but the task of recalling these bitter memories is odious, and I stop midway
They might, perhaps, be forgotten,—they might, at least
have vanished from the popular memory, had they had no

successors. But what Irish boy has not conversed with men who saw crimes as shameful and inhuman committed in Wexford and Carlow at the end of the last century? Crimes for ever renewed cannot be forgotten; they are indispensable materials of history, for they have largely contributed to form the Irish character as it exists at this day.*

The Pope sent a nuncio to aid the Irish with his advice and with some help in money and arms. Luke Wadding, founder of the Franciscan Monastery at Rome, which in many a troubled day, in after times, reared priests true like him to the cause of Irish nationality, was their Agent with the Holy See. Irish officers returned in considerable numbers from France, Italy, and Spain, and brought, we may assume, a deposit of arms which, according to an English

---

* Leland describes an incident of another character in the war worthy to live as long as the story of Regulus.

"The Romish bishop of Ross, who had been particularly active in raising and animating these unfortunate troops, was taken prisoner in the engagement. A man so distinguished in his opposition to the parliamentarians could expect no mercy; Broghill, however, promised to spare his life, on condition that he should use his spiritual authority with the garrison of a fort adjacent to the field of battle, and prevail on them to surrender. For this purpose he was conducted to the fort; but the gallant captive, unshaken by the fear of death, exhorted the garrison to maintain their post resolutely against the enemies of their religion and their country, and instantly resigned himself to execution. His enemies could discover nothing in this conduct but insolence and obstinacy, for he was a Papist and a Prelate."

spy, these gallant exiles had long before "bought out of the deduction of their pay," in hopes of some such opportunity. Richelieu meditated sending officers and money, perhaps, a French expedition to Ireland, when death cut short his great career. The war continued for seven years; but it is not possible in a bird's eye view of our history to follow it into detail.* In the end the success of the Confederates, and his own repeated defeats in England, induced Charles to open negociations with the Catholics and propose terms securing them religious liberty, and a fair share of political power in their own country. The faithlessness which marked his whole career, however, lost him his last friends. He was impatient for Irish help to regain his position, but he meant to buy it a bargain. "I do " therefore command you" he wrote to the Lord Lieutenant, " to conclude a peace with the Irish, whate're it cost, so that " my Protestant subjects there may be secured, and my " regal authority preserved. But for all this, you are to " make the best bargain you can, and not to discover your " enlargement of power till you needs must; and though I " leave the managing of this great and necessary work " entirely to you, yet I cannot but tell you, that if the " suspension of Poining's Act for such bills as shall be " agreed on between you there, and the present taking away

---

* The story is told with great spirit and careful research in Father Meehan's History of the Confederation of Kilkenny.

"of the Penal laws against Papists by a law will do it,
"I shall not think it a bad bargain, so that freely and
"vigorously they engage themselves in my assistance
"against my rebels of England and Scotland, for which no
"conditions can be too hard, not being against conscience
"and honour."

His Lord Lieutenant at this time was the head of the great Anglo-Norman house of Butler. Lord Ormond was a man of excellent capacity, but cold, greedy, unsympathetic, and of doubtful faith; for he gorged himself with plunder in the end at the expense of those whom he wooed to become partisans of the king. He had been converted to the religion of the Court, and regarded the creed he had abandoned, with a contemptuous dislike. The Butlers for four centuries had been sly, watchful, accommodating courtiers, Englishmen in Ireland rather than Irishmen, and the Great Duke, as he is sometimes named, was the supreme type of his race.

The Catholics who remembered Charles's double dealing about the "Graces" were not prepared to pay him in advance a second time. If they set him up again in England, he must set them up in religious and political equality in their own country. It was a fair proposal; but so little was Ormond disposed to second it that he gave up Dublin to the Parliament (on excellent terms for himself personally), and left the country rather than assent. The

King, after a little sent him back to Ireland, with such private instructions as we may surmise from what ensued. Pressed by his increasing danger in England he despatched a Catholic nobleman to the Confederation bearing an affectionate private letter from Charles to the Nuncio, and a public despatch conceding all that was asked. But the unhappy, faithless prince at the same time privately wrote to Ormond, "Be not startled at my great concessions to Ireland, for they will come to nothing." The royalist party in the Confederation, consisting chiefly of those who would never have taken up arms, if they had not been so effectually goaded by Parsons, were for trusting to Ormond, and putting their strong places and their armies at his disposal. But Owen Roe was of a different mind. He understood the King and his Lord Lieutenant, and with a mistrust of their promises, which we now know to have been well founded, declined to fall into these views. A large Ormond party soon shewed itself in the Confederation; distracting cabals and counter cabals sprung up; and no one on either side stands quite free from blame except O'Neill. His is the one name that still lives in popular love and traditional reverence. The people of his day recognised, and their posterity recognise, the essential difference between such a man, and the faction of Irish royalists. They were fighting for the King, for their class, for court favour, for promotion and plunder; Owen Roe was fighting for his country. The line dividing right and wrong, which is so visible now in the perspective of history, was sometimes obscured indeed by the haze and dust of conflict, but it was more fatally obscured by the blindness of faction to which the Celtic nature too readily lends itself.

In the end Charles preferred throwing himself on his kinsmen the Scots; who, being a practical people, handed him over to the parliament, on condition of a prompt settlement of certain arrears of pay. Owen Roe, dissembarrassed of the King, won a memorable victory over a parliamentary army, at Benburb. The loss of the Puritans, mostly Scots, with Ulster planters for auxiliaries and led by the ferocious Munroe, was prodigious. More than twenty officers were killed, and as many as 3,200 of the rank and file; over thirty standards, and the great guns, ammunition, and equipment of a camp, fell into the hands of O'Neill; whose loss, in killed and wounded, did not amount to quite two hundred men.

A dismal period follows Benburb; during which the Confederates, instead of using the victory to consolidate their power, were broken into two parties; one for the king (who again changed his mind, and eagerly sought the aid of the Catholics on their own terms), and the other, like the English parliamentarians, determined to put no more trust in him, and to stand out for National independence.

During these dissensions a fatal calamity befell the Irish cause in the sudden death of Owen Roe.* After that event the war, maintained through seven stormy years with varying fortune, prospered no more. The Catholics, though they still held the chief towns in Munster and Connaught, attained none of the objects for which they were in arms. But let us remember that though unsuccessful, they were fighting for freedom of conscience, as the Scots at the same time were fighting for it; as the Dutch, somewhat earlier, had fought for it. They did not succeed in escaping from bondage, but the wrath of their keepers at the attempt deserves the sympathy of mankind in the same measure as the rage of a slave-driver whose tranquillity has been disturbed by unexpected resistance to the lash.

When Charles was deposed and executed, Cromwell carried his victorious army across the Channel to conquer Ireland for the Commonwealth. His campaign was as coldly merciless as was Alva's in the Netherlands, or Carew's in Desmond. We are assured on high authority that he was in truth a humane and beneficent ruler, who only struck hard because it was necessary to execute divine justice on the authors of the Ulster Rising. In pursuance

---

* It was widely believed that Owen was poisoned by a treacherous gift from a Puritan lady (after the practice of the previous century), but no evidence to justify this suspicion has ever been exhibited.

of this meritorious policy he besieged Drogheda, which was held for the king, and put to the sword the entire garrison, and the population of all ages and both sexes; nobody being spared. The massacre continued for several days; it is admitted that between three and four thousand persons were butchered in cold blood; and a score or two of the inhabitants, who alone escaped, were sent as slaves to the tobacco plantations. Among the garrison was an English regiment, commanded by an English Cavalier, and as Drogheda always lay within the English Pale, where the native Irish were long forbidden to inhabit a walled town, the traders and citizens were almost without exception Catholics of English blood. What Cromwell actually did was to kill certain Englishmen and Anglo-Irishmen in order to punish the imputed offence of O'Neills and O'Reillys, Maguires and MacMahons. The account of the transaction which he sent to England was that it was a righteous judgment executed " on the barbarous wretches who had imbued their hands in so much innocent blood." He repeated this lesson of divine justice at Wexford. There the garrison and population were Irish, but Irish of the South; there is no reason to believe that it contained one soldier or citizen who had ever crossed the Boyne, or been any more associated with Sir Phelim O'Neill than with Praise God Barebones. The modern justification for these massacres is therefore somewhat defective in a foundation of fact.*

The English Parliament ordered a general public thanksgiving throughout the whole nation for the happy event at Drogheda. No one will much wonder that they did so; to rejoice in a successful butchery was in accordance with the spirit of the age. But the fact may serve to mitigate the indignation of English critics that a French transaction of the same character was the subject of rejoicing at Rome.

Cromwell was successful in Leinster; but Munster and Connaught were still unsubdued, and even in Leinster there were cities and forts in the hands of the Irish. He only took Kilkenny after an obstinate resistance, and failed to take Waterford. He made a winter campaign in the South without any decisive success, and returned to England, leaving Ireton in command of the army. Ireland was not effectually conquered; there were resources remaining for a national struggle, and the English royalists now placed all their hopes upon that country. The Irish with good reason, distrusted the Royalists, but they were pained and outraged by the execution of the King. His son was urged by his Anglo-Irish partisans to come among

---

* See Cromwell's "Declaration for the undeceiving of deluded people," in a note in the Appendix. The most imaginative of Napoleon's bulletins is not a more deliberate perversion of truth than the proclamation of this Latter-day Saint.

them, and, if he had done so, it is probable that Royalists and Catholics, in their temper at that time, would have rallied round him. He preferred relying on his countrymen the Scots, who accepted him as their King, on conditions which made him infamous, and destroyed his last chance in Ireland. He had to subscribe the Covenant against Papists and Prelatists, and to publish a declaration acknowledging his father's sin in having married his mother—"an idolatrous woman"—and in having made peace with the Irish Papists; which peace since his father's death, he had himself acknowledged and confirmed. When these proceedings became known there was an end to the royal cause in Ireland. Charles took the earliest opportunity to send private assurances to the Catholics that he only made these professions for convenience, and under duresse; but his father had exhausted this device, and garrison after garrison submitted to the commonwealth.

Irish officers, who surrendered on terms, got permission to embody regiments, and carry them into the service of any country not at war with England. By this politic measure the fighting men who might endanger, or at any rate might disturb, the new settlement, were got rid of at a stroke.

The troops of the Confederation, during the entire war, did not put one man to death in cold blood. The troops of the Parliament, when the contest was practically at an end, shot general officers, as if they were banditti—among others the son of Owen Roe, and Heber MacMahon, Bishop of Clogher, who succeeded Owen as commander-in-chief. Of rank and file, they slaughtered, during the War, ten times the number who had fallen in the Rising. And there are incidents in that remorseless campaign which might move the pity of Robespierre or St. Just. A commission was issued to bring to condign punishment, the instigators and leaders of the Rising; but the long war had already destroyed them, and the only notable victim of the commission was Sir Phelim O'Neill.*

---

* Sir Phelim has left a bad reputation, and was undoubtedly a merciless enemy. But England had the rearing of him; he was educated by the Court of Wards. There is a story (in Leland) of the treatment of an ancestor and namesake of his own, two reigns earlier, which, perhaps, may help to account for his savage disposition.

"A solemn peace and concord was made between the Earl of Essex and Phelim O'Niall, however, at a feast wherein the Earl entertained that chieftain; and at the end of their good cheer O'Niall and his wife were seized; their friends who attended were put to the sword before their faces; Phelim, together with his wife and brother, was conveyed to Dublin, where they were cut up in quarters. This execution gave universal discontent and horror."

At the close of the war, Sir Phelim fell into the hands of the English, and his death proved that he was not wholly wanting in noble qualities. As he stood on the gallows, "Colonel Hewson answered, that he might save his life if he pleased, only by declaring at that moment to the people, that his first taking arms was by virtue of a commission under the broad seal of King Charles the First: but Sir Phelim replied that he would not save his life by so base a lie, by doing so great an injury to that Prince. 'Tis true, he said, that he might the better persuade the

Cromwell was now undisputed master, and a period followed which we are exhorted to recognise as the sole era when an authentic God-given ruler made divine justice prevail in the land. Of his divine government of Ireland the naked facts are these: Two years after the war was at an end, and when the fighting men of Ireland to the number of 40,000 had been encouraged to take service with Spain, he drove out by beat of drum the entire Catholic population of three provinces, excepting only hinds useful to hold the plough or herd the flocks of the conquerer Aged men and women, feeble and sickly persons, many who were protected by general treaties, others who were protected by special terms of submission, some who had received personal guarantees for personal services, were driven across the Shannon, to find a shelter if they could in the bogs of Connaught, and their lands divided among his soldiery. Peers and knights who had fought for the king, to whom they had sworn allegiance, were held by the representative of divine justice to have incurred this penalty. If they returned they became liable to be hanged without trial.* Of the labouring

---

people to come unto him, he took off an old seal from an old deed, and clapt it to a commission that he had forged, and so persuaded the people that what he did was by the King's authority, but he never really had any commission from the King."—Carte's *Ormond*.

 * That all England approved of these measures was a matter of course. With many great and generous qualities there is to be found in

classes all who were considered dangerous, were treated with a barbarity beside which Louis Napoleon's deportation of his political enemies to Cayenne, in our own day, was mild. They were seized upon, and sold into perpetual slavery in the West Indies, at so much a head; five and twenty pounds being the average price which the Commonwealth obtained for an Irish slave. Twenty thousand men, and a large number of women (said to be chiefly the wives of soldiers who had been induced to enlist in foreign service), were so transported and sold. Youngsters, who cannot be considered guilty of any offence, shared the same fate. By the direct agency of Cromwell's son a rape like Herod's, was committed on the children of the poorer classes, of whom he caused 1,000 boys to be sold as slaves and 1,000 innocent Irish girls to be sent to Jamaica, to a fate which would scarcely be adequately avenged if the

---

Englishmen a singular promptitude to hate those who thwart them, and sometimes a savage sternness in dealing with enemies who have given no immediate or commensurate provocation. The cruelty of Cromwell, though inordinate, can scarcely be regarded as exceptional; for a hundred years later the unoffending French Catholics of Acadia were dragged from their homes without notice and flung on a strange shore without preparation or resources. The soldiers engaged in this infamous task so far from being moved to pity, could scarcely be restrained from murdering the innocent strangers.* Longfellow, in Evangeline, has painted the scene in colours that will not fade; but he has appealed only to our pity, suppressing what would move our wrath and horror.

* Bancroft's *American Revolution*, Vol. I., page 232.

authentic ruler spent an eternity in the region to which Cavalier toasts consigned him. The admitted aim of the Lord Protector was to extirpate the Irish race, and his policy is still known among them as the "Curse of Cromwell." If this be indeed the art of divine government, it was afterwards practised more successfully in the *fusillades* and *noyades* of the French Jacobins, and in the Bulgarian atrocities painted by a modern statesman; and it reaches its perfection in the management of a prize by pirates, when the crew are made to walk the plank, and the booty distributed among the victors. Cromwell's conduct is still defended on the same fanatical pretences employed to justify the expulsion of the Huguenots from France, the Moors from Spain, the Jews from England, and the Christians from Japan, and the grounds are good for all these transactions, or for none of them.*

---

* The difficulty of harmonising the opinion of the two nations, respecting representative men, is not less striking in this era than in any that preceded it. The inspired eyes which saw the heavens opened could discern nothing but evil in Irish Catholics fighting for liberty of conscience, or in Irish Presbyterians when they were troublesome to Cromwell. The author of "Robinson Crusoe," born to delight the youth of all nations, makes it a bitter reproach to Oliver that he abandoned the scheme he had under consideration to expel the whole Irish race from Ireland. The transactions of this period have been the subject of furious controversy for more than two centuries. The story was first told by men who were sharing the plunder of the Irish after their defeat, or by servants of the English Parliament, instructed to justify the policy of their employers. In our own day the malignity of Borlase and

They claimed to be pre-eminently Christian, these Puritan soldiers and statesmen—the only God-fearing men, a great historical critic affirms, to be found in that distracted era. But the Christianity they professed is distinguishable by wide differentia from the doctrine of the Founder. It did not teach them to love their enemies, but to abhor and exterminate them; nor to do good to those who hated or thwarted them, but to do them all possible evil. Examined closely the honest fanatics, and the sombre intriguers for power of that era, who proscribed all opinions and practices except their own, are seen to bear a singular resemblance to the men of the same mixed motives, who, a hundred years later, in a neighbouring country, suppressed religion, royalty, and rank as essential vices, and flung innocent women to the scaffold or to the devouring sea, with an indifference as stoical as Cromwell's in sending them to the slave sheds, or the harem of a Barbadoes planter.

One of the Puritan soldiers has left us a picture of Ire-

Temple seem to have revived in Mr. Froude, but critics unconnected by race or religion with the old Irish, notably Mr. Lecky and Mr. Prendergast, have examined the evidence with scrupulous care; and students who desire to understand the period thoroughly, may consult with great advantage the "History of England in the Eighteenth Century" of the former, and the "Cromwellian Settlement" of the latter. They have defended the character of their country (before an unfriendly audience for the most part), with a generous courage which recalls the memory of Grattan and Curran.

land under the rule of the Saints, which bears small resemblance, it must be confessed, to the New Jerusalem "The plague and famine had so swept away whole counties that a man might travel twenty or thirty miles, and not see a living creature, either man, beast, or bird, they being all dead, or had quitted these desolate places. Our soldiers would tell stories of the places where they saw smoke, it was so rare to see smoke by day, or fire or candle by night."*

Before Cromwell's policy was carried to complete success the Restoration brought back the Stuarts. Charles II. having compensated or reinstated a host of royalists ejected from their estates in England, turned his attention to Ireland. The enemies of his house were in possession of the lands confiscated under Cromwell, and the friends of his house, the original proprietors, who were the last to lay down arms for his father, some of whom had shared his own exile, were in penury and destitution.† It was a

---

* Col. Laurence, one of the Cromwellian officers.

† The king who never said a foolish thing, and never did a wise (or honest) one, was ready enough to acknowledge the service of the Irish, if that would suffice. "In the *last* place we did, and must always remember, the great affection a considerable part of that nation expressed to us, during the time of our being beyond the seas, when with all the cheerfulness and obedience they received and submitted to our orders, and betook themselves to that service, which we directed as most convenient and behoofeful, at the time to us, though attended with inconvenience enough to themselves, which demeanour of theirs cannot but be thought very worthy of our protection, justice, and favour."

case needing prompt handling, and Charles handled it
with unusual promptitude. To pacify the Irish Puritans
he confirmed the settlement of property under the Commonwealth. That is to say, Cromwell had given to his
soldiers the estates of the Catholic gentlemen who had
fought for the house of Stuart, and the restored house of
Stuart graciously confirmed the arrangement. Charles
would certainly have preferred doing justice, if justice
could be done without much personal inconvenience. But
he loved his harlots and jesters too well to run risks; and
to do justice in this matter was made difficult by a sentiment always powerful in England; a sentiment which has
created a perpetual barrier between the two nations, and
which while it exists will never suffer them to unite. His
English parliament, crowded with Cavaliers and returned
exiles, would not have helped him to displace Englishmen,
though they were Cromwellians, to make place for Irishmen, though they were Royalists. His impulse to do
justice was at best not very strong; a slice of confiscated
land remained at the disposal of the Crown, with which
he might have made a provision for a few more of the
worst cases of injustice; but his heart was touched with
fraternal affection, and he gave the bulk of it—a hundred
and seventy thousand acres and upwards—not to Irish
sufferers, but to his brother James.* Although the

---

* There were nearly 8,000,000 acres to dispose of without interfering

Cavalier parliament did not give back their estates to its Irish allies, it is needless to say that it did not quite overlook them. It compelled the king to withdraw a rash indulgence by which they were permitted to practise their religion. It passed a Test Act, by which no person could

---

with Cromwellian occupation. Two millions and a quarter were given to Irish in possession, Irish of English descent, Irish declared innocent, or saved under provisions in the Act of Settlement; to English courtiers or soldiers there were given four millions and a half. James got a great slice of the remainder, and Ormond almost as much. At first it was proposed to treat the Irish with some approximation to fairness, and to restore the lands of all who had made peace with the King. But it was feared this concession would cut too deeply into the Cromwellian confiscation, and there were whispers of a Puritan revolt in Ireland, which might, happily, spread to the other island. Charles made haste to assure the discontented that their title should be confirmed, and thereupon they embraced his cause with enthusiasm. Some who had helped Cromwell to mount his father's seat, Charles elevated in rank, or endowed with fresh plunder, notably Lord Inchiquin, Lord Broghill, and the heir of Sir Charles Coote. As the valorous steadfastness and stern veracity of the Puritans is a theme upon which we have heard long discourses, it will be profitable to note that in return for a secure title to their estates, the Irish Puritans cheerfully denounced in the next Parliament the "abominable usurpation" of Cromwell from whom they obtained them, and lamented the "traitorous murder" of the royal martyr, whom they had helped to lead to the block. On Charles' conduct in this transaction Hugh Reilly, the Irish Chancellor of his brother, James II. makes a reflection which must be recognised as just and natural: "That the King should not only pardon and reward the rebels upon their returning to their duty, but reward them with the birthright of such as adhered to him to the last, with the hazard of their lives and limbs, against those very rebels, is so unaccountable a procedure, that we can find no precedent for it in any history, sacred or profane."

hold any office, civil or military, without subscribing a declaration against transubstantiation; and as bullocks from Meath and Kildare brought down the price of fat stock in the English market, it declared the importation of cattle from Ireland to be a public nuisance. In another session the business was clenched by an act prohibiting the introduction of these objectionable animals for ever; whether "dead or alive, great or small, fat or lean." Some members who objected were assured with the gracious courtesy reserved for Irish debates, that none "could oppose the bill but such as had Irish estates, or Irish understandings."

This was the reign of the "Merrie Monarch," a time of national enjoyment and revelry in England, interrupted only by an English Popish plot and massacre, more deliberate and bloody than the plot and massacre in Ulster, over which history is so clamorous. The plot was the famous invention of Titus Oates; the massacre, the trial, conviction and murder of his victims for eighteen months; whose execution went on merrily long after the time when judges and juries had ceased to believe a syllable of the evidence. These victims were English Catholics, because the inventors of the plot probably knew nothing personally of the Irish; but that Ireland had no share in a conspiracy to restore Popery, was so improbable that the patrons of the plot in London insisted on Irish victims. Oates and his comrades might make inconvenient blunders; but the Privy Council ordered the Lord Lieutenant to make proclamations for persons fit for the work. All who could make discoveries relating to Ireland were invited to come in without delay, and threatened with penalties if they were dilatory. There were at that time living in the country three men whom crime and want had made fit competitors with Dangerfield and Bedloe. They were living as cattle stealers and robbers, some of them liable to capital charges, but the character of witness of the plot was equal to a protection under the privy seal. One was a suspended priest, the others apostate friars, who had been expelled from their communities. These men charged Oliver Plunkett, Primate of the Catholic Church, with having conspired to bring in a French expedition, and to levy an Irish army to aid them. His trial was ordered to be held in Dundalk; but as he was well known to the jurors, and the whole community there, no witnesses appeared when his arraignment took place. But this difficulty was overcome; he was carried over to London, tried before an English jury, and on the ordinary incredible evidence of the period, convicted and executed.* If the Catholic king,

---

* At the same time the Archbishop of Dublin, a Talbot of Malahide, then suffering from a painful disease, was committed a prisoner to Dublin Castle by Lord Ormond, and kept there for two years till he died of want of air and exercise.

who soon followed, had been strong and merciless as Cromwell, if he had slaughtered the judges, juries, and spectators of this massacre, and their contemporaries indiscriminately for the offence of being alive at the period, if he had sent men in thousands to be slaves in the West Indies, and women to a worse fate, he would be qualified to-day, doubtless, like Oliver to be recognised as a benevolent agent of Divine justice.

When James II. embroiled himself with his English subjects by attempting to make changes by royal prerogative, which could only be legitimately made by Act of Parliament, he sought support in Ireland. The Irish never loved James, they knew him chiefly as a plantator in Tipperary, but his present offences were not such as could reasonably be expected to move their indignation. He was a Catholic and he sought to extend religious liberty to Catholics and Dissenters. If his method was harsh and arbitrary, the boundaries of royal prerogative were ill-defined, and nations have never been slow to condone offences committed in their own interest. A little later the strictest Scottish Whigs forgave William for suspending statutes by his royal authority in Scotland; though suspending statutes by royal authority was the offence for which his predecessor had been driven from the throne. The laws in operation against his fellow Catholics indeed were such as a reasonable man could not justify, or a humane man endure. The religion of the State was guarded with more than Mahomedan rigour. It was a capital offence to receive a member of the dominant church into the Catholic faith. It was a capital offence for a member of the Society of Jesus to land on the soil of England. In the great Universities founded by Catholic piety no Catholic could hold an office. In the army which Catholic nobles had led to victory on so many memorable fields no Catholic noble could hold a commission; no Catholic peasant could carry a musket. To modify these barbarous laws was the clear duty of one having the authority and responsibility of a prince. If James had endured them without resistance he would have been known to posterity as the basest of the long line of English kings. But he undertook his appointed task in the worst spirit. He was headstrong and arbitrary, and yet easily deluded. He counted on impunity because he believed the incredible doctrine preached from the pulpits of the English Church since the Restoration, that the duty of a subject was non-resistance to the will of his prince in every extremity, and he determined to do by authority and force what he might have succeeded in effecting by persuasion and influence.

James selected as Lord Lieutenant in Ireland, Richard Talbot, the head of an Anglo-Norman house which still remained Catholic, created him Duke of Tyrconnell, and gave him his confidence in a degree unusual to his frigid nature. Talbot is credited with a plentiful catalogue of vices by English writers. It is probable that he was boastful and profligate, and perhaps unveracious, but he was certainly bold, resolute, and devoted to his master, and to the nation he was sent to rule. We must judge him by his age and his contemporaries. He was far from being so unscrupulous a partisan as Shaftesbury, the spokesman of resistance in England, and he was a generous and chivalrous gentleman compared to the hero of Blenheim and Malplaquet. When a conspiracy to bring in the Prince of Orange began to be talked of, Talbot disarmed a large number of Protestant gentlemen, whom he suspected of sympathy with William, and armed and regimented the native population whom he knew to be friendly to James.* What else indeed was an agent

---

* The new levies under Tyrconnell are described by Lord Macaulay as a terror to Protestant innkeepers; they swaggered into taprooms, drank freely, and probably paid irregularly, being but irregularly paid themselves. In truth they were no better nor no worse than the ill-disciplined soldiers of that age, but the judicious reader will get a valuable light on the system on which Anglo-Irish history is written, if he notes that while no excuse can be found for these Irish recruits, English soldiers under identical circumstances are defended and justified. "The pay of the English and Danes (says the same writer,) was in arrears. They indemnified themselves by excesses and exactions for the want of what was their due, and it was hardly possible to punish men with severity for not choosing to starve with arms in their hands."

of James to do? The Protestant gentry were for the most part heirs of Cromwellian settlers, and hated James as a Papist, and feared him as a king who might call in question the title to their estates. They themselves had taken much stricter precautions; when they were in power, a Catholic was not permitted to possess the simplest weapon of defence; half-a-dozen Catholics meeting in Dublin or its neighbourhood constituted an illegal assembly, and in country districts Catholics were not allowed to leave their parish except to attend the neighbouring market. In periods of alarm the precaution has been taken by every Government in Ireland before and since; but so singular are the canons of criticism applicable to Irish affairs, that Lord Macaulay, who was a Cabinet Minister under Queen Victoria in 1848, when arms were taken from Munster Catholics and distributed among Ulster Orangemen, treats this precaution of Tyrconnell's as a grave and exceptional offence.*

---

*One of James' brothers-in-law, Lord Rochester, was his Prime Minister, as far as such a functionary can be said to have existed at that time; and the other, Lord Clarendon, son of the historian, he sent to Ireland as Lord Lieutenant. Clarendon was a submissive, but not a zealous, agent of James' policy. He hated Tyrconnell, with whom of old he had a malignant feud. He despised the Irish, and could not understand why the king troubled himself with their paltry affairs. During his residence in Dublin he transmitted to his brother, the prime minister, constant budgets of gossip and slander, prompted by his

The principal employments, civil and military, in Ireland, were necessarily bestowed on native Catholics. "The highest offices of state, in the army, and in the Courts of Justice (groans Lord Macaulay) were with scarcely an exception filled by Papists."* It was an intolerable grievance certainly, in a Catholic country, under a Catholic king, who had only a handful of Protestant partisans in the island, that Catholics were so employed. To be sure, in England when James's opponents got the upper hand, the highest offices of state, in the army, and in the courts, without a single exception, were filled by Protestants, but that was "*bien différent.*" While the Prince of Orange, in correspondence with some of James's Privy councillors and generals, was collecting on the coast of Holland an army of Dutch, French, and German troops to invade his kingdom, the king summoned to his aid a portion of his army in Ireland, recruited like the army of his father in a large part from Irish Catholics. An army similarly recruited has since won memorable victories for England in Spain, Belgium, and France, in Africa, Asia and Australasia, but the proposal was received with a roar of indignation, and a deluge of libels. At the same time two Irish judges, one

---

national and individual prejudices, and it is on this correspondence, in a large degree, that Lord Macaulay has founded his history of Irish affairs at that period.

* Macaulay's "*England,*" Vol. II., p. 70.

of them recognised even by unfriendly critics as the foremost man of his race, were sent to London to make certain representations respecting the condition of Ireland. These officials would have been received with distinction at Versailles or the Escuriel; in London, the mob surrounded their carriage with burlesque ceremonies, among which potatoes stuck on white wands were conspicuous. The favourite jester of the present day,* who ordinarily pictures an Irishman as a baboon or a gorilla, is scarcely more delightfully humorous; and the perversity of a people who do not love such charming pleasantries, has naturally been the perplexity of English writers down to our own age.

While James was meditating a flight to France, some good friend of the revolution indulged in a playful device of a more practical sort. A crowd of fugitives, whose dress bespoke them ploughmen and labourers, rushed into London at midnight, shrieking the dreadful news that the Irish army were in full march on the city, burning houses and slaughtering women and children in their course. Letters containing horrible versions of this Popish atrocity were delivered in distant and widely sundered districts of the country at the same time. The citizens rose and armed in self-defence, and as no enemy appeared they

---

* Mr. Punch.

passed the time agreeably in sacking and burning the houses of Catholic gentlemen and tradesmen. The enemy never appeared, and the story turned out to be a pious fraud; a partisan of the Whigs afterwards claimed the merit of having schooled the shrieking fugitives with his own lips, and written the letters with his proper hand. The good bishop who saw the Protestant ghosts clamouring for an avenger in the broad day light, on the bridge of Portadown, or the ingenious scribes who furnished the daily bulletins of the Massacre manufactured in London, scarcely deserved better of the state. Had he lived in our day he would probably have exercised his imagination in kindred pursuits, and become an eminent historical critic.

James fled to France and left his enemies in possession of England and Scotland. In Ireland Tyrconnell held the country for the king, and sent him advice to head a French expedition to Dublin, where he would be loyally welcomed and reinstated in a kingdom. Louis XIV., gave him officers, arms, ammunition and a little money, but no soldiers; and with this poor provision he landed at Kinsale in the spring of 1689. The Irish received him in triumph; installed him in Dublin Castle, the traditional seat of authority, and the best men of the race tendered him their service. A parliament was summoned. It necessarily consisted almost exclusively of Catholics. The Protestants elected amounted to about half a dozen. The

Protestant peers who answered the king's summons reached about the same number, including three Protestant bishops; but small as the number was, it was certainly in excess of the proportion of Protestants in the country who supported James. And it was liberality and generosity compared to the practice it superseded. Up to the coming of James, and throughout a great part of the seventeenth century, an Irish Catholic found it as impossible to get elected to the legislature of his native country as an English Catholic does in the nineteenth. There was but one Catholic in the Irish Parliament of Charles II. The Government was chiefly Catholic also, though James had several English Protestants in his Cabinet, but they were necessarily the minority. Lord Macaulay is disgusted at the number of O'Neills and O'Donovans, MacMahons and Macnamaras who thronged the benches of the Commons; a phenomenon as amazing as to see Russells and Stanleys, Smiths and Brownes, in the parliament of Westminster. Other modern writers have made the scanty representation of the minority a subject of reproach. How the Irish Catholics could have been so bigoted as to prefer entrusting their interests to men of their own race and faith is amazing, to writers of a nation who two centuries later, out of five hundred and fifty representative of England, Scotland and Wales do not elect a single Catholic gentleman.*

---

* The peculiar and exceptional law to which Irish transactions are

The Irish parliament of James has been a standing target for slander down to our own day. Suddenly called together among a people who had slight experience of parliamentary forms, and who had grievous wrongs to redress, they conducted themselves with singular moderation and good sense. They created an army and a navy, they established religious equality among all Christian creeds, they made vigorous efforts to foster native manufactures, and asserted the fundamental doctrine which the English and Irish parliaments reaffirmed a century later, that the Kings, Lords, and Commons of Ireland were alone entitled to legislate for that country.* This Catholic

---

supposed to be subject is a marvel. James took his government from the ranks of his supporters for the most part. "It was now," says Lord Macaulay in a fine burst of indignation, "impossible to establish in Ireland a just and beneficent government; a government which should know no distinction of race or creed." This it seems was the sort of government which it was incumbent on James to set up in Ireland in the seventeenth century. In England a different system of equity was doubtless proper, for the noble historian records with entire approval, that all James's appointments of Catholics to office were immediately cancelled by William and Mary, that English peers who had become Catholics were committed to the Tower for high treason, that before James had reached Calais the Popish priests were in exile or in prison, and no monk who valued his life dare show himself in the habit of his order, and that finally Irish soldiers were not permitted to remain in England; in short that distinction of race and creed was the cardinal point on which the action of the administration in England turned.

* Grattan rejoices that the "Catholics, before taking the field, extorted from James their Magna Charta—a free constitution."

parliament did not pass any law inflicting penalties on Protestants for their opinions. Their fathers had been mercilessly persecuted by the Puritans; they themselves and their children were soon to be mercilessly persecuted under a daughter of the king for whom they were in arms. Their fellow Catholics in England and Scotland at the moment were under hereditary proscription, but they set an example of moderation and forbearance nearly unique in history. The tithes paid by Protestants were ordered to be paid to the Protestant clergy, the tithes paid by Catholics to the Catholic clergy; an arrangement which bears a favourable comparison for substantial justice with a settlement of the same question made in our own day. They did not deprive Protestants of arms, or the franchise; they did not exclude them from parliament or the learned professions; they did not forbid them to acquire or inherit property, or to educate their children in their own faith, nor tempt them by bribes to conform to the religion of the majority. These were wrongs which they did not inflict, but which in the end they were destined to endure. It is true they restored to the lineal heirs the estates which Cromwell a generation before had taken from them. But they accompanied the measure with compensation to innocent persons. In restoring the estates they followed the example of the English parliament. Under Charles II. a few years before the estates of bishops and nobles sold by the Long Parliament at fair market prices, were resumed without any compensation to the purchasers, and the bishops and chapters reinstated in them.* When William was established in authority the same course was taken with the estates of Irish Catholics and Jacobites. It is indeed the course which any government or legislature in Europe at the period would have inevitably pursued. But in James and his Irish Parliament, it was a proceeding for which historical critics can find no conceivable excuse.

The Protestants naturally sided with William. It furnishes a significant commentary on the fatuity of human schemes that the towns and fortified places in Ulster, which James's grandfather had established to maintain his authority, were now strongholds of William. The gates which James I. raised at Derry, Coleraine, and Enniskillen, were shut in the face of James II. The transaction most honourable to the Protestant minority in all their annals is the fortitude with which they held Londonderry for

---

* "Property all over the kingdom was now again changing hands. The national sales, not having been confirmed by Act of Parliament, were regarded by the tribunals as nullities. The bishops, the deans, the chapters, the royalist nobility and gentry, re-entered on their confiscated estates, and ejected even purchasers who had given fair prices. The losses which the cavaliers had sustained during the ascendancy of their opponents were thus in part repaired."—*Macaulay's* History of England, Vol. I., chap. 2.

more than three months against the arms of James. Neither the most painful destitution, nor the most favourable terms could shake their constancy.

James, with the assent of his Irish Parliament, published a declaration of Indulgence, under which Dissenters and Catholics were authorised to practice their religion without hindrance. But royal proclamations cannot tranquilize in a moment a country disturbed by hereditary feuds and bitter wrongs, inflicted and endured. That a populace who had never seen justice or moderation practised, who had just escaped from a grinding and insolent oppression, should commit some excesses when they caught their tyrants at a disadvantage, is precisely what was to be expected in any community. Lord Macaulay, who makes the gossip of the worst enemies of the Irish the basis of his narrative, affirms that certain Protestant clergymen were insulted and even cudgelled in the streets of Dublin by the Catholic soldiery and rabble, and that the ecclesiastical rulers of the University (who were permitted to remove in safety and remain at large) were subject to the hard condition that no three of them should assemble together. He is very vehement in his condemnation of these unpardonable excesses and severities. But the reader must understand that they were only unpardonable when they were committed by Irish upon English, by Catholics upon Protestants. Before James had landed at Calais the Scotch Presbyterians treated the Episcopalian minority, who had long domineered over them, worse than Tyrconnell treated the Puritan minority in Ireland. The Privy Council at Edinburgh ordered all suspected persons to be immediately disarmed; the mob, upon a judicious hint doubtless, took upon themselves to thrust out of their manses all clergymen who had acknowledged episcopal authority. This sport, which was called "rabbling," spread over the entire country, and two hundred ministers were in a few weeks successfully "rabbled;" to wit, kicked, hustled or dragged out of their houses, and beaten or ducked when there was any special provocation. Holyrood, which under a Catholic king had become a Catholic seminary, was stormed and sacked, and the library and vestments of the priests made a bonfire.* The Scotch parliament followed the Scotch rabble, and ejected every minister and every office-bearer in the University who did not agree with the theology of the majority.

---

* In London it was still worse than at Edinburgh. A Catholic priest had to face not only the rabble but the law. It is confessed that he could only show himself at risk of his life for fear of the former, and the latter sent him to the jail and the gallows. Peers who had become Catholics were thrown into the Tower on a charge of high treason, Catholic chapels and the private residences of Catholic gentlemen were wrecked as soon as the flight of James made the sport safe, and the religious orders were everywhere hiding or flying for their lives from an infuriated mob.—(Lord Macaulay's account of the Rabbling in Scotland will be found in the Appendix).

Lord Macaulay makes a reflection on these proceedings, which is very just, only it appears not to have struck him as applicable to Ireland. "We ought to remember (he says) that it is the nature of injustice to generate injustice. There are wrongs which it is almost impossible to repair without committing other wrongs, and such a wrong had been done to the people of Scotland in the preceding generation." What one learns indeed from the historical critics of greatest authority in our time, respecting these transactions, is, that for Scotland to reject the English ritual with horror, and to expel its ministers from church and glebe with scorn and fury, was right and even heroic; but that for Ireland to do something much more moderate was unpardonable persecution.

There is one Act of James's Parliament which is presented to the judgment of mankind, in the declamatory rhetoric of Lord Macaulay, as a measure without parallel in the history of civilized countries. It was an Act of Attainder by which a list of persons named in the schedule, exceeding two thousand in all, were required to appear before the King's Courts in Dublin on days specified, on pain of high treason; a penalty which involved the forfeiture of life and property. Lord Macaulay is emphatic in describing the impossibility under which many of them lay of complying with the law, and the consequent duplicity of the entire proceeding. To less prejudiced critics it may well seem that the Act, under the circumstances of the case, was moderate and merciful. The men who framed it were the heirs of territory snatched from them on fraudulent pretences in the Plantation of Ulster, by bribed judges and terror-striken juries under Strafford, by beat of drum under Cromwell, and by a mere brute act of authority under Charles II. It was directed against peers and gentlemen who, on James's arrival in Ireland, had been summoned by proclamation to attend on him in person—the condition on which they held their lands as Crown tenants. They did not obey the summons; some of them, on the contrary, were in actual arms against the king, and others had, since the Dutch invasion, fled to England to abet his enemies. The confiscation of property belonging to rebels in arms, or to persons acting in concert with armed rebels, is not a proceeding without parallel, but the ordinary practise of all civilized and uncivilized countries. And in this case it was fenced round with saving qualifications honourable to the National Government. The estates of persons who left Ireland since the coming of William were not forfeited, but vested in the Crown till they had an opportunity of justifying themselves. And it was provided that proprietors absent from sickness, or other reasonable cause, if they returned at any future period should be restored to their possessions; the rents being employed during their absence for the support and defence of the kingdom. The Attainder of upwards of two thousand persons was a hard act; but it was one so entirely in the spirit of the times that when William obtained the upper hand he outlawed nearly four thousand of James's partisans, and divided upwards of a million of acres of their estates among his soldiers and favourites. The same practice continued down to our own day; and sometimes the penalty was imposed under conditions completely identical with the conditions in the Act of James.*

James's policy was not national but personal; it was mainly directed to placate his opponents, and gratify his friends in England. Lord Macaulay considers that this, indeed, was the sole end James ought to have kept in view, and that he pursued it too fitfully, owing to the resistance

---

*In the reign of George III., for example, an Act was framed by the Executive of that sovereign in Dublin, and received the Royal Assent on the 6th of October, 1798, identical in spirit and purpose with the Act of James's Irish Parliament, in every essential, except the number of persons on whom it operated—a purely accidental circumstance. It required fifty-one persons named to surrender before the 1st of the ensuing December on pain of high treason; a penalty which, as in James's time, involved the loss of life and forfeiture of their property to the Crown. The men whose surrender, within six or seven weeks, was rendered compulsory were notoriously in France, where news from Dublin only penetrated by chance, and where all facilities for return were suspended by a war with England. If it be answered that they were in France because they were rebels to the authority of the Crown in Ireland, this is precisely the answer James was entitled to make respecting a multitude of the names in his Act of Attainder.

of his Irish counsellors. Some of his Catholic advisers in
London could see no necessity for restoring their plundered
estates to the Irish, and these honest gentlemen history
recognises as "good Englishmen." But his Irish counsellors represented a force which was the chief factor in
the case ; and if they staked their lives and fortunes, and
the fate of their country on the issue of the contest, they
might reasonably desire that a victory brought some better
result than setting up anew the gallant Cavaliers who, a
generation earlier, had signalized their return to power by
proscribing religious liberty in Ireland, and pronouncing
the importation of Irish cattle into England a public
nuisance. There is nothing in the proceedings of that era
more gratifying to note than the circumstance that the
Irish leaders held in check the arbitrary will of the king,
and made the despot of England a constitutional ruler in
Ireland.

The supply of gold from France soon ran short. The
precious metals were scarce in Ireland, and James had recourse to the dangerous, but unavoidable, device of coining
debased money. Had he established his authority permanently, the true standard, it may be presumed, would
have been restored, and the base coin issued from the mint
would have returned to the treasury in the payment of
taxes. But as it was immediately made a legal tender,
and employed in discharging obligations of every character,

and as his authority was not permanently established, it wrought great injustice. His memory has suffered sorely from this transaction. It is true indeed that, a hundred years earlier, Elizabeth, also, was compelled by the cost of her Irish wars to pay her troops, for a time, in debased money. But students must take notice that that was a temporary mischance of a great queen, which good men deplore and forgive; while in James it was a crime which it is proper and loyal to stigmatise in charter toasts down to our own day.

In the contest which now ensued, the whole Irish race flew to arms. A larger proportion of the people crowded to the camps of James than any nation in any extremity had ever before furnished for a national war. But there was no adequate supply either of arms or officers; and without arms and officers numbers are merely an embarrassment. The French ambassador and other friendly strangers declare that they were a peasantry singularly endowed with the physical qualities which make good soldiers, but long oppression had lowered their self reliance and self respect. They were of the same race which had fought with Bryan and Art, Hugh and Owen, but the evil influences which undermine national character had been at work among them for more than ten generations. Their lands had been given to strangers; their fathers could be robbed and murdered with impunity as "mere Irish:" to

K

have their goods spoiled and their homes dishonoured by soldiers bearing the king's commission was a common experience down to their own day; and the legends of treacherous kidnapping and secret murder done by the authority of successive Lords Deputy in earlier times was as familiar to them as the achievements of Nana Sahib are to men of the present age. They had not been permitted to learn the use, or enjoy the protection, of arms, except such rude weapons as can be easily made, and easily concealed. Many of them did not know how a musket was charged or discharged. A race richly endowed by nature outlives and recovers from inflictions like these, but their immediate effect is certain to be a decay of intelligence and self reliance. The younger gentry on whom commands necessarily devolved, had no training, and had, indeed, never seen a battalion or a company except (at such distance as one may fancy) the troops kept in Ireland to maintain English authority. With the aid of the French officers, and the few Irish soldiers, like Sarsfield and the Hamiltons, who had seen service in England, it was hoped that these loose levies might be turned into an effective army; but, for this purpose, time was of all things the most necessary. And William understood the importance of allowing no time for such a purpose Ten thousand men—Dutch, French, and English—were despatched to Ireland under Schomberg, the most renowned soldier in Europe at that day. He landed on the friendly coast of Ulster, and attacked Carrickfergus, a small fortified town in Antrim; the garrison after a week's siege capitulated, on condition that they should be allowed to depart unharmed. But the descendants of the plantators, the "imperial race," as their eulogists named them in contrast to the Celts, understood so little of the usages of civilized war that they rose in great numbers to murder the disarmed soldiers; and were with difficulty restrained from a general massacre by the personal exertions of Schomberg. The incident, it must be confessed, might have happened at that day among any population who saw their hereditary enemies suddenly placed at their mercy. But when excesses occur among the Irish it may be noted that, in English chronicles, the perpetrators figure as barbarous savages, yielding to their native instincts; whereas among the Anglo-Irish or Scoto-Irish they are attributed to the natural heat of a population exasperated by insolence and wrong.

Schomberg proceeded by slow marches to Dundalk, the frontier town between the northern and eastern provinces, but lying within the boundary of the latter, and there fortified himself. James marched out of Dublin to offer the invader battle; but the experienced veteran did not consider his army in a condition to fight a pitched battle. He shut himself up within his lines and trained his new

levies in military exercises. The season was unusually
rainy, and his intrenched camp became an Irish bog. His
only veteran troops were French Huguenots, and some of
them became so discontented with their position that they
opened communication with the French ambassador in the
camp of James, with a view to change parties, and were
only restrained by military execution, and close imprisonment from actual desertion.* The English, mostly new
levies, were unfit to encounter the privations and severities
of a life under canvass in an Irish winter, and died in
multitudes. He was at length forced to retire into Ulster
without striking a blow, having lost half his troops by cold
and pestilence. In the beginning of the summer of 1690
William himself sailed for Ireland with large reinforcements. He landed in the North, and found himself at
the head of a powerful army well furnished with artillery,
clothing, stores, and all the necessaries of war. He had
invaded England at the head of a muster of Swedes, Swiss,
and Batavians, commanded by Huguenots and Dutch-
men, with a handful of English malcontents and refugees
to make a show of national support. His Irish army was

---

* Lord Macaulay suggests that these traitors were probably not
Huguenots but French deserters from the army of Louis in Flanders
who masqueraded in the character of Huguenots. I have never had an
opportunity of investigating the facts of the case, and on such a question
Lord Macaulay is an unsafe guide.

as heterogeneous. It consisted chiefly of English recruits, supplemented by the Dutch and Huguenots who had accompanied Schomberg, and by German and Scandinavian veterans hired for the war. A regiment of horse and a regiment of foot raised by the Ulster Protestants, constituted the only national element. James's army had had also been reinforced. King Louis sent him 6,000 trained soldiers, under the command of a French general, in return for four Irish regiments whom he took into his own service; but his native troops were still imperfectly supplied with arms, stores, and artillery, and some of the regiments were almost in rags. The numbers of the opposing forces are variously stated; it is reasonably probable that the Irish army did not reach 30,000 men, while William's army closely approached 40,000. James's advisers were of opinion that, under the circumstances, he should garrison the great towns, retire behind the Shannon, and postpone a pitched battle till further supplies of arms and officers arrived from France; but he was impatient for a decisive result, and overruled them. William marched towards the capital, and the Irish barred his way at the Boyne, a fordable river twenty miles from Dublin. There a decisive battle took place on the morning of the 1st of July; and the larger numbers, with better discipline and equipment, handled by the skill and experience of the most renowned soldier in Europe, carried the day.

The French regiments were guarding James's army from
a flank movement, and had little share in the fighting;
the Irish foot, ill armed, ill clothed, and undisciplined,
could not hold their ground against veteran troops selected
from half the armies of Europe, but the Irish horse, it is
admitted on all hands, performed extraordinary service.
They checked William's advance so effectually that when
night closed he had not gained above six miles of the road
that led him to the capital, and his renowned general had
fallen on the field which he won. James, who watched
the battle from the Hill of Donore, overlooking a wide
landscape, fled to Dublin long before it had terminated,
carrying away a regiment of Irish horse to protect his
sacred person. The bulk of his troops retired on the
capital in good order. He had still an army at his disposal, and behind the army a nation; but he lost heart
and fled to France.*

---

*Lord Macaulay, and other critics following in his train, represent
the triumph of the English as the necessary and inevitable success of a
superior race contending with an inferior one. The larger battalions,
the foreign allies, the veteran troops, the concentrated power in the
hands of an organized government, and the renowned general disappear
from view, and one hears, only, of the destiny of an imperial people.
But it is worth remembering that wherever the superincumbent force of
numbers has been for a moment removed, and a fair field created, in
India, Canada, or Australia, for example, the competition of the Celt
with the Anglo-Saxon accords ill with this disparaging comparison.
The party of William succeeded, and it is inferred that they necessarily

William got possession of Dublin and took immediate action to strengthen his position. The train bands of the capital were purged of all Papists, and it was ordered that only Protestants should be permitted to serve in them thereafter. This was a judicious precaution, and must not be confounded by a heedless reader with the action of Tyrconnell in disarming Protestants, which of course admits of no excuse.

The Irish, disencumbered of James's timid and meddlesome counsels, stood gallantly at bay. The French officers recommended them to capitulate, but they would not hear of submission. Patrick Sarsfield, afterwards Lord Lucan, a grandson of Roger O'Moore, and as dear to his nation as his great ancestor, took a lead henceforth in national counsels. He was a trained soldier, having served with credit in the English army, and a generous patriot, and he possessed the physical gifts which charm the popular eye. He advised and led the Irish in another campaign, distinguished, chiefly, by his own brilliant services. They maintained

---

deserved to succeed. The strength which asserts itself by actually governing, we have been assured in later times, is a sufficient evidence of the right to govern; without relation to the relative strength of the parties.* A rule which, it may be presumed, applies to the case of a baby-farmer who starves his nurslings, or a costermonger who jumps on his mother. If not, why not?

* Froude's *English in Ireland*.

themselves for twelve months in Munster and Connaught
against the skilful soldiership of William and Ginkel, till
they were able to make an honourable capitulation at
Limerick. The siege of that city is a story of gallantry
and devotion embracing all classes, and both sexes of the
besieged. But the Irish annalists record with greatest
pride an incident that marked its close. Before the city
was actually delivered up the arrival of a long-promised
expedition from France, with men, money, and arms, was
announced; but Patrick Sarsfield, who was in command,
considered his honour and the honour of his race engaged
in completing the surrender, and completed it accordingly
with a French fleet lying in Irish waters.

There was great rejoicing in England; Ireland bowed
her head in the dust. It is the misfortune of the two
nations that their interests were never identical. If in
England James was a despot conspiring by illegal processes
to subvert the Constitution, in Ireland he was a Deliverer
coming to set up law and liberty. Had he succeeded in
establishing his throne among a people with whose religious convictions he would have had no temptation to
meddle, resting on the support of a parliament which
under great temptation showed itself to be just and
moderate, he might have become an inoffensive and perhaps
a useful ruler, and the whole course of Irish history would
have been changed for the better. The landed proprietors

would have lived at home, and have had no inducement to carry their income and their ambition to another country. The natural resources of the island would have been gradually employed in creating national wealth; its best intellect and highest soldiership and statesmanship would not have been wasted on foreign countries, and one of the bloodiest pages in human history would never have been written.*

The treaty of Limerick guaranteed to the Catholics the same exercise of their religion, which they had enjoyed under Charles II., and the maintenance of property as it existed at the date of the instrument. The bulk of the Irish army withdrew to France with Sarsfield; a handful who remained lived as disbanded soldiers have lived in every country, by scanty supplies from friendly natives and predatory levies off unfriendly settlers. The new government gave them a fine lesson of humanity and moderation, for "every kern that was caught was hanged without ceremony on the nearest tree."†

---

* The Irish attribute the loss of the Boyne to James's panic; but a conquered army are apt to require a scapegoat. When he arrived in Dublin, the first-comer from the battle field, he saluted Lady Tyrconnell by exclaiming, "Madam, your countrymen have run away;" to which the high spirited lady replied, "If they have run away, your Majesty seems to have won the race." He is still spoken of in Ireland as "*Shamus a Cack*," a title which will not bear to be translated.

† Lord Macaulay. Mr. Froude puts the fact more graphically. "Noted Tories were shot like goats among the crags."

William's parliament took back the estates restored to the Irish owners, and reinstated the Cromwellian settlers or their heirs. If the reader desires to be in harmony with the verdict of English history on these transactions, he must be careful to discriminate, for that verdict is a little puzzling and contradictory. It was right under James I. to take away the land from the undoubted owners in Ulster, but it was an atrocious outrage for the owners or their heirs to reclaim it. It was right and righteous of Cromwell to confiscate two more provinces. It was politic and proper under Charles II. to confirm this new confiscation by his enemy (though the contrary course was taken at the same time in England) and it was shameful and even fraudulent in James's parliament to reinstate the original owners. But it would not at all have been wise or just for William to have followed the example of Charles II. and confirmed the settlement made by his predecessor. On the contrary, he was clearly bound to drive out the owners once again. If a reason why be demanded, the reader is to understand that the improvements made by the English settlers created a title superior to the original ownership. They claimed by the right of a higher civilization—a plea which, if it be good, would justify Paris in seizing upon London, and London in seizing upon Liverpool or Glasgow. But he must not fall into the error of supposing that if the Puritan settlement in Ulster or Munster had been a French settlement in the weald of Kent, or if the chances of war had enabled Baron Haussman to plant boulevards and open a Rue de Dorking in Westminster, that the principle would be applicable in such cases. It is only in force in Ireland.

The advantages secured to Catholics by the Treaty of Limerick were moderate. But when the flower of the Irish army had withdrawn to France, and the remnant could be hanged without ceremony, they began to look inordinate. The parliament of Cromwellian settlers and Government officials in Dublin having excluded Catholic members, by requiring from them an oath of abjuration, in direct infringement of one of the articles of surrender, were free to proceed at their discretion. They first passed a stringent statute depriving Catholics of arms, and another ordering all " Popish archbishops, bishops, vicars-general, deans, jesuits, monks, friars, and regulars of whatever condition to depart from the kingdom on pain of transportation," and then proceeded to consider the treaty. They discussed it in the spirit of a gang of banditti considering how much they can extract, by way of ransom, from a prisoner ; and resolved by a decisive majority not to keep the conditions affecting the Catholics. William, who had promised his Catholic Continental allies to establish religious liberty, and who had confirmed the articles of surrender with his own hand, struggled for a time to preserve his honour; but it is not convenient for a new king to be in conflict with his friends, and after a time he gave way. If the canons of public morality were not as we know suspended in the case of Ireland, the house of Nassau would lie under another imputation in this business, not less dishonouring than the judicial murder of John de Barnevelt or the massacre of the MacDonnells of Glencoe. The justification of the "Glorious Revolution" is that William was entitled to drive out James, because James employed his prerogative and influence to give the Catholic minority undue advantages in England. When William employed his prerogative and influence to give the Protestant minority undue advantages in Ireland, he committed the identical offence which he professed to abhor and avenge; unless, indeed, human justice be a municipal law, restricted in its operation to the island of Great Britain. In Ireland the treaty of Limerick can never be forgotten; it is one of the title deeds of the Irish race to their inheritance in their native land.

For more than a century its sordid and shameless violation was as common a reproach to England on the Continent, as the partition of Poland has been a reproach to Russia in our own day. It will not be necessary, however to have recourse to the censure of foreign critics, or the recrimination of plundered Catholics, to understand the transaction. An Act was at length passed styled "An Act to confirm the Articles of Capitulation at

Limerick," and its character is described in a Parliamentary record of permanent authority. The more moderate of the conquerors, and some malcontents who got none of the plunder, made a stand for public justice, and having failed to amend the bill, entered a protest on the journals of the House of Lords signed by ten peers and four bishops of the Irish Establishment. This protest declares that not one of the articles agreed upon between the King and Sarsfield was fully confirmed; that while it was the manifest intention of the treaty that they should be confirmed in favour of those to whom they were granted, the pretended confirmation placed the Catholics "in a worse position than they occupied before." That words were inserted in the Act which were not in the Articles, and material words in the Articles were omitted from the Act, whereby their meaning and intention were altered. That one important clause which affected the liberty and property of the Catholics was altogether omitted. And as this anxiety about justice to conquered Catholics might seem a little unreasonable and ill-timed, the document terminated by declaring that certain Protestants who had purchased property, or accepted mortgages, on the faith of the Articles, would be seriously injured by the breach of public faith committed in the measure.

Had this transaction happened in France, and the wrong been inflicted on the Huguenots, it is not improbable that

the critics who have taught us to abhor the bad faith of the
Bourbons and Bonapartes, would have discovered another
suitable text for moral indignation. But the ordinary
English reader has not heard much of the capitulation of
Limerick. Still less does he know that the disregard of
public faith carried its punishment along with it ; of which
he has not altogether escaped a share in permanent public
taxes. The bigotry which by revoking the Edict of Nantes
drove an army of skilled artisans out of France, did not
prove a more disastrous blunder, than the bigotry which
by repudiating the articles of Limerick drove a hundred
and fifty thousand Irishmen into the armies of France
during three generations ; soldiers who, under Louis le
Grand and the first Napoleon, baffled the policy of England,
and changed the history of the world at Fontenoy and
Austerlitz. The names of great Irish soldiers emblazoned
on the walls of Versailles, among " *les officiers genereux
morts pour la France,*" and of statesmen and diplomatists
buried in cathedrals and colleges from Vienna to Madrid,
and of a host of less conspicuous names carved in cloisters
and vaults in Rome, Louvain, Douai, Salamanca, and
Valladolid, represent a formidable force transformed by
bad faith into irreconcilable enemies.

The more spirited and aspiring of the Catholic gentry
from this time forth sought foreign service. In every
Catholic state on the Continent they won distinction in

arms and diplomacy. The suckers torn from the ancient Celtic stem struck roots so deep in friendly soil that, in our own day, after the lapse of five generations, their descendants have occupied offices of authority in every Catholic country in Europe, and the foremost place in three great empires, Austria, Spain, and France. Irish colleges and monasteries were endowed in Flanders, France, Portugal, and Spain, and in the capital of the Christian world, chiefly by the earnings of these exiles. most of which subsist to this day.*

---

* Before quitting the reign of William it is proper to warn students against putting faith in the picturesque romance which Lord Macaulay has produced by way of a history of James's transactions in Ireland. Irish history has often been written (and, unhappily, is still written) by furious partisans, and shameless libellers, but their gross inventions are not so exasperating as the plausible, moderate-seeming, persuasive misconstructions of Lord Macaulay. His account of Talbot's viceroyalty, for example, is as effectual a perversion of fact as any writer with pretentions to fairness was ever guilty of. He requires from him a forbearance and moderation of which there is no instance in his era, in England or elsewhere. The age was far from being one to train a man in sentimental humanity. When a boy, Richard Talbot had personally witnessed some of Cromwell's brutalities in Ireland; in his manhood he had seen Shaftesbury, with great nobles of England at his back, sending batches of innocent men to the hangman, to promote a purely personal interest. His own kinsman, the Archbishop of Dublin, stifled by a long imprisonment in Birmingham Tower, was one of their victims. Yet he killed nobody in return. He took away arms from men who would use them to overthrow his master, and gave them to men who would use them to sustain him. But for the offences, real or imputed,

When Anne succeeded William the minor provisions of the treaty, spared in the first instance, were one after another set aside by law. The Catholics were reduced to a condition closely resembling the bondage which black slaves endured in the southern States of America. They were excluded from Parliament, from the magistracy, from the army, navy and public service, from the bar, and finally from juries, and from the franchise, all of which they had possessed under Charles II. The nobility and gentry continued to seek a career in Catholic states; and the class who remained in Ireland and the children they reared were disabled from disturbing the supremacy of the conquerors by being reduced not merely to poverty, but to the worse bondage of ignorance. Education was forbidden.

---

of Irish politicians, Lord Macaulay can find no excuse. It would seem as if they stood alone in history, or at any rate in British history. Yet nobody knew better than he that the ministers of the Restoration who brought in Charles, and the ministers of the Revolution who brought in William, the statesmen who helped George III. to oppress America contrary to their convictions, and the mercenaries who helped him to subvert the policy of his ministers, and defeat their measures at his discretion, were among the basest of mankind. Nobody knew better that if one sought worse examples of shameless want of public and private honour than prevailed in London, he must go not to Constantinople, but to Edinburgh, at almost any time while Edinburgh continued the seat of a subordinate Government. For these humiliating facts, there are various palliations and excuses doubtless, of which the historian duly reminds us; but palliation and excuses are forgotten when the case of Irishmen is under judgment.

To become teacher in a Catholic school or tutor in a Catholic family was a felony. To establish or endow a Popish school was strictly prohibited, and no Papist could become an usher in a Protestant school. Many youths were sent to foreign colleges, and to check this abuse Catholics were forbidden to leave the country under heavy penalties.*

Religion was more fiercely repressed. That no more priests might be ordained, all bishops were banished; and with them all the religious orders. To return, or to introduce any foreign priest, was made a capital offence. The secular priests already in Ireland, were permitted to remain on obtaining a licence from the Government, but after a little this permission was subjected to the impossible condition of swearing that the Pope had no spiritual authority in Ireland. The priest who abandoned his vows, and renounced his faith had a provision made for him at the cost of the state. The means of necessary self-defence were taken away. Catholics were deprived of arms, and

---

* "One statute prohibited a Papist from instructing another Papist; another prohibited a Protestant from instructing a Papist; a third provided that no Papist should be sent out of Ireland to receive instruction. If these three laws had duly been capped by a fourth, ordering for execution every Papist who neglected to provide a first-class education for his children, the whole edifice would have been beautifully complete and symmetrical."—Lecture by Professor J. W. Barlow, M.A., Professor of Modern History in Trinity College, Dublin.

excluded from the militia; but a paternal sovereign
enabled them to participate in the patriotic services of this
force by paying twice as much as Protestants towards its
support. They could not build or arm vessels of war for
the defence of their coasts ; but if the Pretender or any
Catholic prince invaded them, the duty of making good the
injury inflicted was assigned exclusively to them. They
were forbidden to purchase or inherit land, or to hold it as
lessees, except on a limited and imperfect tenure. Children
were encouraged to become informers against their parents,
by a right of succession granted to any child of a Catholic
who conformed to the State Church ; the betrayal of a
Popish father or guardian being in the eyes of Parliament
equivalent to baptism and confirmation. If none of the
children conformed the estate at least was broken up; on
the owner's death it was divided among his sons in equal
parts. The bulk of the nation were from that time a sort
of tenants-at-will in their own country. But it is easier
to enact a penal law than to enforce it. A few Catholics
saved their estates by the aid of Protestant friends, for to
the credit of human nature there were always individuals
more generous than the law. In the monasteries and
bourses established for Irish students on the Continent, a
succession of priests of Irish birth or blood were trained
to face the savage rigours of the Penal Code. They found
their way to Ireland in disguise, and lived the lives, wore

the dress, and endured the privations of peasants, to keep alive the faith of the nation. The persecuted race loved God, acknowledged the mercy of his chastening hand, and clung closer to the creed for which they had made so many cheerful sacrifices. The prayer and incense ascending from a thousand altars in the great Cathedrals of Christendom, did not, to my thinking, furnish a spectacle so sublime and touching as the Mass solemnized under the dripping roof of a cave, among a crowd of rugged peasants, —the unconquerable remnant of a brave and pious nation —by a priest who served God at the constant peril of his life.

The Puritans hated the natives with the same pious scorn with which the Castilian hated the Moor, and they were encouraged to indulge this passion without stint; but otherwise they were treated as vassals by the Crown. The population, whether Cromwellians or Catholics, were subject to the rule which long prevailed in all British possessions throughout the world, that the dependent state only existed for the benefit of the paramount state. If they wove their wool into broadcloth, they were not allowed to carry the fabric to any market but England. If they preferred to sell the raw material they were not allowed to sell it in any market but England. The flock-owners smuggled it a good deal to France and Spain, and their lawlessness has not escaped bitter reproach. But they still find apologists in Ireland who insist that a bench of bishops, or the twelve apostles, would have smuggled under the circumstances.

The submission of the Undertakers to the Crown was abject. There was the name of a parliament in Dublin, under William and Anne, but neither the spirit nor substance. The Senate of the Lower Empire, or the Senate of Louis Napoleon would scarcely have endured the humiliations to which they meekly submitted. In contrast to the patriotism of James's Parliament, they consented to declare that Ireland was "dependant on the Crown of England;" and on the question of native manufactures they became the mere agents of English rivalry and greed. Woollen fabrics had been a successful industry among the Celts since before the Invasion; they were greatly prized in France and Italy in the early ages, and though the industry had passed, with so many other of their possessions, to the Anglo-Irish, it still maintained a prosperous local and foreign trade. Yorkshire became jealous, and, at its instigation, the House of Commons in London called upon William to discourage this manufacture in Ireland; with a significant intimation that his doing so was the only alternative to laws which would "prohibit and suppress it." The Deliverers sent a bill to Dublin, loading Irish woollens with a destructive export duty, and the Parliament of soldiers and Undertakers, whose Protestant constituents were the persons mainly interested, passed it into law. But this was not enough. The law might be violated, and Irish jurors might not regard the offence of sending Irish woollens to the markets of France or Spain as altogether unpardonable, and an Act was passed in London which provided that if an Irish jury failed to convict a person charged with the offence, he might be seized and carried to England, and tried there anew—where the result could not be doubtful.

All their relations with the larger island were regulated on the same principle. They were prohibited from trading with the Colonies, and no colonial produce could be carried into Ireland which had not first been landed in an English port, and yielded a profit to an English trader. Live cattle, as we know, had long been excluded as a nuisance; the graziers tried salt meat as an alternative, but it was speedily prohibited; even hides—a raw material which English tanners were eager to obtain—were forbidden, lest the interest of land owners, who were paramount in parliament, should suffer. They had still the linen trade; but liberal bounties were granted on English and Scotch linen to compete with it, and Irish sail cloth, which had found favour with the national and mercantile marine, was loaded with duties which proved completely prohibitory. Even the sea was forbidden to them; fish caught on the Irish coast could be carried only in English bottoms manned by English sailors. As they could not export wool, the land owners desired to export corn, and a bill to promote tillage was prepared in Dublin; but it was sent back from the Council in London, with an intimation that the design could not be permitted, as the exportation of Irish corn would prejudice the English trade. They might import what they pleased from England indeed, and among the imports was a steady stream of candidates for all the best employments in Church and State, of which the garrison were unblushingly cheated. This was the price which Irish Protestants paid for the luxury of oppressing Irish Catholics. The interest of the Catholics in the business was of the slightest. The Penal Code, designed to cut up industry and frugality by the root, provided that if any Papist presumed to cultivate his farm so successfully that it produced a profit greater than one-third of the amount of his rent, it might be claimed by the first Protestant who reported the offence, and they had no corn to export.*

The design of planting the island with foreigners was not lost sight of. Every batch of adventurers for five hundred years had brought back the same enticing story —a country beautiful to see, delightful to dwell in, and

---

* Perhaps this legislation may enable Englishmen to understand why the Celts were not more industrious and frugal, they were restrained by law from indulging in these British virtues.

where noble settlements might be made as fast as the Government rooted out the natives. When the supply of English settlers was exhausted, Protestant immigrants were brought from Germany and France. But the system of government, for the exclusive gain of England, disgusted the foreigners, and they either abandoned the country in despair, or remained to rear Irish rebels for the next generation.

The Protestants of the capital, who were of the religion of the court, and the Protestants of the Plantation, who were for the most part Presbyterians or Puritans, agreed ill. The courtiers detested the perversity which rejected bishops and deans, and might, it was suspected, on slight provocation come to reject kings and nobles. The Established Church denied the validity of Presbyterian marriages, constantly troubled them in the exercise of their faith, and deprived them by Episcopalian tests of a fair share in the ascendancy they had helped to win. The planters who had long kept watch and ward against the "mountainy men" despised the worldlings who spent their lives in witnessing stage plays and ungodly dances, or in intriguing for employment and favour in the Castle yard; and were never sorry to see Church or king in a little trouble.

Among the Catholics there was no national literature, no books of any kind indeed except a few pamphlets

written by Irish priests or exiles on the Continent, and
smuggled into the country. But an injured people have
a long memory. By the fireside on a winter night, at
fairs and markets, the old legends and traditions were a
favourite recreation. The wandering harpers and pipers
kept them alive; the itinerant schoolmaster taught them
with more unction than the rudiments. Nurses and
seamstresses, the tailor who carried his lapboard and
shears from house to house, and from district to district,
the pedlar who came from the capital with shawls and
ribbons, the tinker who paid for his supper and shelter with
a song or a story, were always furnished with tales of the
wars and the persecution. An historian, already frequently
quoted, cannot repress his disdain that in those times—
for this was "the Augustan age of Queen Anne"—no great
drama or epic poem or masterpiece of art was produced in
Ireland; but it is not on the gaolers in this penal settlement,
but on their prisoners that the critic's reproaches fall.*

Under the House of Hanover the penalties got gradually

---

* Mr. Froude's contempt of a people who did not sing with the robber's knife at their throat, is not intrinsically more malign than an opinion which Lord Macaulay volunteers "that the Irish Catholic suffered nothing which he would not himself have inflicted," a *dictum* which would have as much support from fact if it were employed to justify Nero's persecution of the Christians. When the laws of Anne were proposed, a Whig official of that era may claim to rival Lord Macaulay in the nature of his sympathy with the wronged. Three eminent

modified. The Irish Catholics took no part in the risings in favour of the Pretender ;* the memory of the Stuarts was stained with bad faith and selfishness, and of all the

---

Catholics were permitted to be heard at the bar of the Commons against the first bill, and they made a case worthy in its gravity and pathos of the spokesmen of a nation. They were answered (by Lord Macaulay's predecessor) that if they suffered penalties the fault was their own ; let them conform to the religion of the State, and there would be no penalties ! Mr. Hallam judges the era more justly than his brilliant competitor. "To have exterminated the Catholics with the sword, or expelled them like the Moriscoes of Spain, would have been a little more repugnant to justice and humanity, but incomparably more politic."— (Constitutional History.) But for sympathy and moral indignation one must go to a foreigner. "The sad and patient Judea (says Michelet), who counted her years by her captivities, was not more rudely stricken by Asia. But there is such a virtue in the Celtic genius, such a tenacity of life in this people, that they subsist under outrage, and preserve their manners and their language."

* The Irish on the Continent, however, took a decided part in the attempt. "The Waterses, father and son (says Mr. M'Gee, in his History of Ireland), Irish bankers at Paris, advanced one hundred and eighty thousand livres between them ; Walsh, an Irish merchant at Nantz, put a privateer of eighteen guns into the venture ; Sir Thomas Geraldine, the Pretender's agent at Paris ; Sir Thomas Sheridan, his preceptor, with Colonels O'Sullivan and Lynch, Captain O'Neil, and other officers of the brigade, formed the Staff. Fathers Kelly and O'Brien volunteered in the expedition. On the 22nd of June, 1745, with seven friends, the Prince embarked in Walsh's vessel, "The Doutelle," and landed on the northern coast of Scotland. . . . From that day until the day of Culloden, O'Sullivan seems to have manœuvred the Prince's forces. At Perth, at Edinburgh, at Preston, at Manchester, at Culloden, he took command in the field or in garrison ; and even after the sad result he adhered to him with an honourable fidelity which defied despair."

Stuarts James was the most odious; but though quiet at home, the Irish Brigade had recently won the battle of Fontenoy, and it was discreet to tolerate them a little. Priests who could furnish the surety of two freeholders for their peaceful conduct, and did not outrage good taste by showing themselves in public, were permitted to perform their functions in bye streets, and back places. Provided always that they were careful to ring no bell, and erect no steeple, these indulgences being absolutely incompatible with the safety of Church and throne.

The policy of the Penal Laws, it must be admitted, was entirely successful. There remained a Catholic people, but no Catholic nation. A host of historical families disappeared, and the few Catholic peers and gentry who retained some fragments of their ancient property, were never heard of outside their demesnes. A hundred years after the battle of the Boyne a Catholic merchant pleading for Emancipation, declared that there was no longer any reason to fear a claim to the forfeited estates, as the descendants of the ancient possessors had sunk into the dregs of the people and were labourers in the fields or porters on the quays of Dublin, or beggars in the streets unable to read or write, or prove their legitimacy, or trace a pedigree.* No institution remained to hold together the

---

* Speech of John Keogh at a Catholic meeting in Fishamble Street Theatre, March 23, 1792.

fragments of the Irish race except the national Church, which had braved constant persecution, and humiliation, which is harder to bear than persecution, to watch over its flock. The Catholics, like the Jews, excluded from political life, threw their energy into trade, and a race of successful merchants at length arose, who began in the time of George III. to make some claim to their natural rights. Their claims got listened to by statesmen and thinkers, but made no impression on the mass of English opinion, till circumstances forced upon the Government in London the necessity of bidding for their sympathy.

The need of conciliating the Catholics arose in this fashion. From the moment William got settled on his throne the more discerning of the Anglo-Irish began to claim for themselves all the rights enjoyed by Englishmen in England, and the claim was renewed under Anne, and the two first Georges. But it was ill supported by the middle class, and was generally regarded with wrath and scorn by the great nobles, who inherited confiscated estates, and were still Undertakers and jobbers at the mimic court in Dublin. It is curious that the sons of English officials should have furnished the most courageous and successful advocates of Irish nationality, down to the era of O'Connell. Early in William's reign William Molyneux, son of an officer of the Irish Exchequer,

son-in-law of an Irish Attorney-General, and himself
member for the University of Dublin, and sometime
in employment under the Crown, first formulated the
constitutional claim of Ireland as a separate and independent Kingdom, united, but not subject, to England,
"annexed but not conquered." As Molyneux was a man
of scholarly pursuits, and the principal founder of a local
school of philosophical inquiry, his "Case of Ireland"
excited immediate interest among the cultivated classes.
It was dedicated to the Deliverer, and founded on the
principles of the Revolution. It contained nothing,
indeed, which did not afterwards receive the assent of
Parliament in London and Dublin, when Irish opinion
became strong enough to insist upon a hearing. But
the doctrine had to encounter the common fate of
new truths. The English Parliament pronounced it
to be a seditious libel, and ordered the tract to be
burned by the common hangman. It is probable
that they would have proceeded to treat the author
in the same spirit as his performance, but that
death snatched him from their jurisdiction. Molyneux was the close friend of John Locke, the philosopher
of the Revolution, and it was the fatigue incident
to a visit made to that eminent man in England
which brought on his fatal illness. He died in the prime
of life, and at an era which students will note,

as eight years after the battle of the Boyne, and a century before the death of Lord Edward Fitzgerald.*

A quarter of a century later the same great thesis was revived by Swift. Jonathan Swift, the son of an Englishman in a public employment, was born in Dublin, educated at Kilkenny School and Trinity College, and may be said to have begun his career in Ireland as a Castle Chaplain. He subsequently won a rank in English literature which set him on a level with Addison and Pope, and a place in English politics, nearly unique as the secret counsellor and chosen companion of Bolingbroke and Harley, the Disraeli and Derby of that day. He would probably have become an English bishop, and spent his life as a royal chaplain and political pamphleteer, but that Queen Anne insisted, with some grounds indeed, that he was scarcely orthodox, and refused to promote him to that dignity. She was induced, however, to create him Dean of St. Patrick's Cathedral in Dublin, his orthodoxy being sufficient, it may be presumed, for Irish use; and he returned in middle life to live and die in his native city. When he was between fifty and sixty, he burst into Irish politics with a

---

* Molyneux has left a crux for the bewilderment of British statesmen, which still solicits their attention. "We have heard great outcries, and deservedly, on breaking the edict of Nantes and other stipulations How far the breaking of our Constitution, which has been of five hundred years' standing, exceeds that, I leave the world to judge."—Molyneux's *Case of Ireland.*

"Proposal for the universal use of Irish manufactures," and later with the famous "Drapier's Letters." An English speculator by judicious bribes to a Mistress of George I. (the ugliest and most rapacious of the strange Hanoverian harem which followed him to England when he was brought over to become Defender of the Faith), obtained a patent for coining Irish half-pence, and to make the transaction profitable enough to satisfy all the legitimate and illegitimate claims upon it, coined them, it was asserted, of debased copper. Swift, in a series of letters written in the character of a Drapier—so draper was then spelled—described, and perhaps exaggerated, the loss which would be inflicted on the country. The nation took fire, and the excitement spread to every class of society; the grand juries, the parliament, the courts of law pronounced against the scheme. For the first time, men of all parties, and both religions were of one mind; even the beggars considered themselves in danger of being cheated; for they were exhorted to remember that the ordinary alms in adulterated money would not buy a mouthful of bread or a draught of beer! When the excitement was at its height, Swift raised the question of the political relations, which under the British Constitution ought to exist between the two countries. This special wrong, he complained, had been inflicted on Ireland without consulting the Irish Parliament, which was of right as free and supreme a parliament within the island, as the English Parliament in England. The printer of this dangerous sedition was prosecuted by the Crown, but the Grand Jury of Dublin threw out the bill of indictment; the judges, who were as servile dependants of the Crown as in the time of Strafford, attempted to wheedle the jurors by private remonstrance, but without effect; a reward of £300—a considerable sum at that era—was offered for the discovery of the author, but, though it was as well known who was the Drapier as who was Dean of St. Patrick's, no one would consent to prove the fact. Sir Isaac Newton, then Master of the Mint, appeared in a character, which the greatest Englishmen have not escaped when Ireland was concerned, that of an abettor of wrong. He certified officially the purity of Wood's halfpence.* But it was in vain. The Irish people were unanimous, and the project had to be abandoned. It is a curious illustration of the profound influence which nationality has always exercised over the Irish mind, that Swift, who was only fair to the Catholics by fits and starts, never indeed gave them any help to redress their special wrongs, and who cordially detested Protestant dissenters, was, up to his death popular with the whole nation. When he was supposed to be in

---

* It has been suggested, and it is probable, that Wood sent to Sir Isaac specimens of the coin less adulterated than those in common use.

danger of arrest, the mob of the Liberties followed and watched over him as fondly as they would have watched over O'Connell in a later age.

One may still smile at the scorn, disguised in an irony that strives in vain to be playful, with which Swift treated complaints of Irish ingratitude to England, and of Irish offences generally against the sister country, which were to be heard even in that day.

"I was much delighted, he says, with a person who hath a great estate in this Kingdom, upon his complaints to me, how grievously poor England suffers by impositions from Ireland. That we convey our own wool to France in spite of all the harpies of the custom-house. That Mr. Shuttleworth, and others, on the Cheshire coasts, are such fools to sell us their bark, at a good price, for tanning our own hides into leather; with other enormities of the like weight and kind. To which I venture to add more: that the mayoralty of this city is always executed by an inhabitant, and often by a native, which might as well be done by a deputy with a moderate salary, whereby poor England loseth, at least, one thousand pounds a year upon the balance . . . That the people of Ireland presume to dig for coals in their own grounds; and the farmers in the county of Wicklow send their turf to the very market of Dublin, to the great discouragement of the coal trade at Mostyn and Whitehaven. That the revenues of the Post Office here, so righteously belonging to the English treasury, (as arising chiefly from our own commerce with each other), should be remitted to London clogged with that grievous burden of exchange, and the pensions paid out of the Irish revenues to English favorites, should lie under the same disadvantage, to the great loss of the grantees. When a divine is sent over to a bishopric here, with the hopes of five-and-twenty hundred pounds a year, upon his arrival he finds, alas! a dreadful discount of ten or twelve per cent. A judge or a commissioner of the revenue has the same cause of complaint."

The doctrine of Molyneux and Swift, that the Irish Parliament was of right sovereign and independent, bore no immediate fruits. A lad, still at his first school, when the Drapier's letters were published, arrived at manhood before it was again effectually asserted. Charles Lucas, originally an apothecary, and afterwards a doctor of medicine, who won some distinction in his profession, took up the thesis,. and asserted anew all that Molyneux and Swift had taught. Lucas was a sturdy demagogue of the middle class, vigorous and irrepressible, but narrow and parochial. He desired popular liberty, provided it were jealously restricted to good Protestants. But Parliament was so servile, that to claim freedom, even for Protestants, was to be overbold. Though he was a voluminous writer, he wanted the skill and still more the authority, by which Swift had moved and controlled the whole nation. The Grand Jury of Dublin—whose predecessors threw out the bill against the printer of the Drapier's letters, presented Lucas's writings as seditious, and ordered them to be burned by a functionary of the grim class, who had dealt with Molyneux's treatise in Palace Yard. The Corporation of Dublin, who in our day have placed his statue beside those of Grattan and O'Connell, condemned him as a public enemy; and the Irish Parliament, which, if it were re-

M

assembled, would assuredly inscribe his name on a roll of honour, summoned him to its bar to answer for his grave offences. To avoid immediate imprisonment and more serious penalties to follow, he had to fly to England. After ten years absence, he returned to Dublin, and was elected a member of the Parliament which had exiled him. He took an active and public-spirited part in affairs during the remainder of his life, but Providence denied him the supreme happiness of seeing the seed he had sown arrive at maturity. He died eleven years before the Declaration of Independence, and left behind him the first foundation of a free press in the *Freeman's Journal,* which he established to teach his opinions.*

While Lucas was in exile, the national claim was revived by a man better qualified and better placed to ensure it a hearing from parliament. Henry Flood, son of a Chief Justice, and soon to be allied by marriage with the great governing family of the Beresfords, a man of fortune and rank, and still in the prime of life, entered the House of Commons, and took his place with the small fluctuating Opposition, which, in that day, made some show of defending national interests. Flood was gifted with a powerful

---

* When it is said that he took a public-spirited part in affairs, it must be understood always in the exclusive interest of Protestant Ascendancy. He was bitterly ungenerous to poor Munster tenants who were struggling, in his time, against a grinding tyranny, because they belonged to the creed of which he disapproved.

intellect, and a resolute will, and with manners which were frank and winning. He had been carefully educated, and he found no difficulty in becoming a master of parliamentary practice and parliamentary tactics. His junction with the Opposition had the same magical effect as placing a unit in front of a row of ciphers. The party which accepted him as its leader soon became a power, not only in Parliament, but with the nation. The claim of Ireland to legislative independence was heard again in the press and in society, and became the animating spirit of the Opposition. It would, perhaps, have been in vain to assert the claim by a positive resolution, till some happy opportunity arose. At any rate, Flood proceeded by other methods. The House of Commons was then elected for life; the majority consisted of nominees of the great peers, the heirs of confiscated property, who owned boroughs, and controlled cities and shires, and it was wholly irresponsible to public opinion. Flood at length carried a reform bill, which brought it in some degree under popular control, by limiting its existence to eight years. The first Parliament elected under the new act, expressed its discontent with the Government, by throwing out a Bill of Supply. The Viceroy was as deeply amazed and outraged as Charles I., under similar circumstances. He immediately prorogued the offending Parliament, and did not call it together for more than a year. But during the recess the Opposition kept opinion alive, and alert, and when it re-assembled, he found that Flood was no more to be cowed than Pim. Under his guidance, the House once more rejected a money Bill, and after a time was induced to level a direct vote of censure against the Irish administration. The Viceroy, who in those days, not only reigned, but governed, was recalled, and Flood won a second victory, which like the first, helped to prepare the Irish Parliament, and the Irish people, for the great achievement which they were soon to accomplish.

But Flood committed a mistake fatal to his influence, and long disastrous to the national cause. After an opposition of more than fifteen years, he accepted office with the Executive on which he had so long made war. It has been contended, with some show of probability, that he wished to assert the principle of Parliamentary Government, and to carry liberty another stage, by forcing the leader of the Opposition into power. But, unfortunately, he did not comply with the cardinal condition of such an experiment, by carrying his opinions into power along with him. For seven years, the greatest orator the Anglo-Irish race had then produced, was tongue-tied and helpless, while measures were passed, which promoted as of old, the policy and interest of England, not those of the people which the Parliament he sat in was supposed to represent. At length, in 1781 he threw up his office, and returned to

Opposition. His reception among his old friends was rendered easier by the interposition of the "good old King." George III., in a gust of passion, struck his name out of the list of Privy Counsellors, with his own royal hand; and there could be no doubt that the breach between the great Orator and the Court was serious, and probably final. The party which Flood led, on his first entry into parliament, were known as the Patriots, and, like all parties, it included men of divers characters and purposes, Some of the great proprietors joined it because they were malcontent, or from other motives which at bottom were probably venal and shabby enough. The latest English historian of this era covers them with contempt for bartering their votes for the favours of the Crown, and thwarting the good intentions of the patriot king. A country whose gentry so conducted themselves was, he insists, plainly unfit for parliamentary institutions. Honest Iago! This was under the House of Hanover, when, in the Parliament at London, a succession of Ministers, from Walpole to Newcastle, bought and paid for votes at so much a head, with bank notes handed by the Minister in person to the political prostitutes of the day—men who were not, as in Ireland, aliens misrepresenting the bulk of the nation, but often the best blood of the country. The good king who was thwarted at Dublin, was the same king against whom his most upright servants in England had to keep watch lest, after having consented to a measure in the closet he let loose a gang of hirelings to defeat it in parliament—a gang kept in constant pay for this honourable duty. The same king whom his subjects in the thirteen United Colonies of North America afterwards found themselves under the necessity of thwarting at Lexington and Bunker's Hill. But their offence has not been visited with the destruction of public liberty in their country.

At any rate Flood returned to a party widely different from the one he had left. A dozen years earlier, his most effectual colleague outside Parliament, was Henry Grattan, a young barrister, and son of the Recorder of Dublin. Though there were nearly twenty years difference in their ages, the men of genius acted cordially together, somewhat in the character, doubtless, of teacher and pupil, in the first instance. They not only took counsel on party tactics, but, like Pitt and Canning, in later times, directed the fire of the press against the common enemy.* But when Flood became a member of the Irish Executive, their paths separated.

---

* See Baratariana, a collection of political squibs published in Dublin, in 1773, where Ireland is treated as Barataria, and the Lord Lieutenant of the day, Lord Townsend, as Sancho. Flood and Grattan were the chief contributors. The official and stipendiary defenders of the Government replied to the best of their ability in the *Dublin Mercury*.

Immediately afterwards Grattan was elected to Parliament, and, though still a young man, he had become during the seven years of Flood's secession, the real leader of the Opposition. He was more generous and sympathetic than his friend, and he had possessed the party with more liberal opinions than of old, and with a loftier sense of public duty. They sympathised, most of them, with the struggling Colonies in America, and were prepared to make concessions to the Catholics; and on both points they separated widely from Flood. He could scarcely hope to lead such an Opposition, and could ill endure to serve in the ranks.

The wilfulness of George III. furnished the opportunity for which Ireland had long waited. He required the free colonists of America, who had legislatures and budgets of their own, and who asked nothing from the mother country but good will, to submit to taxation to be imposed on them by the Parliament in London, where they were not represented. They protested and remonstrated with surprising good humour and forbearance; but the claim was persisted in till the thirteen colonies which then acknowledged the authority of the British Crown, were compelled to summon a Congress, and levy an army, for defence of their natural rights. There had been a constant stream of emigration from Ireland to North America for three generations; a movement probably destined to influence the course of its history, in the end, as decisively as the sailing of the Mayflower; and in the Colonial army it was noted that Irish Catholics and Irish Presbyterians were conspicuous. The first opulent gentleman who staked his immense fortune in the contest was an Irish Catholic. The first naval victory was won by another Irish Catholic.* And Irish Presbyterians who furnished a notable number of successful officers, and courageous soldiers, boasted that England was paying at Boston for sins committed at Belfast. Their brothers at home read with pride the names of their kinsmen who were fighting for liberty, and Washington had soon to acknowledge money transmitted from Protestant Derry and Belfast, and a cargo of clothing from Catholic Cork, which reached him at a moment when the fortune of his country stood lowest.

But Ireland was a factor in the contest in a more decisive manner, which has somehow got a good deal forgotten in modern times. The French succours under Lafayette, which at a critical moment turned the scale in favour of America, included three regiments of the Irish Brigade— the regiments of Dillon, Walsh, and Berwick, amounting to between three and four thousand men—"who," says General Arthur Dillon, "claimed, as they always had

---

* John Randolph said: "I have seen a white crow, and heard of black swans, but an Irish opponent of American liberty I never either saw or heard of."—Judge Black, of Pennsylvania.

done, the right to be first to march against the English." General Dillon, who afterwards held a high command under Dumourier in the campaign where the armies of the Republic flung back the force of confederated Europe, did brilliant service in America, and General Conway competed with Washington himself in influence with the Congress.* One can fancy with what passionate interest these transactions were watched in Ireland. They speedily turned the vague sentiment of nationality into a purpose and a passion. A happy accident favoured this new purpose which was stirring in the breast of the nation.

The coast of Ireland facing the Atlantic was swept by privateers bearing the flag of the United Colonies, and Paul Jones, in their name, carried off a prize in the narrow sea between Ireland and Scotland. The eastern coast also stood in need of protection. Privateers commissioned in France, but manned and commanded by Irishmen, preyed on the English ships, which alone were permitted to engage in the carrying trade between the islands. The Irish

---

* The reader will find in the Appendix an extract from a report of the achievements of the Irish Brigade by General Dillon, describing their services in America. The report was made in 1794 to the National Assembly of which General Dillon was a member. It was procured for me by Mr. J. P. Leonard of Paris, to whom Ireland is under so many obligations. The relation of Conway and Washington forms a striking incident in Thackeray's "Virginians," where the Irishman, of course, is placed at a disadvantage.

Executive were unprepared and helpless. They could only furnish " a troop or two of horse, and part of a company of invalids" to defend Belfast, lying dangerously near to the last adventure, and they were compelled to allow that vigorous town to defend itself. They sanctioned the formation of Volunteer corps for the protection of the northern coast, in which a landing had been successfully effected by the French less than twenty years before.* The example spread rapidly over all Ireland, and the Protestant peers and gentlemen who were then supreme, soon found themselves at the head of fifty thousand troops, clothed, armed, and disciplined, without assistance from the State.† Citizen soldiers speedily came to have clear convictions on citizens' rights. It was such a native army which had enabled the American colonists to assert themselves, and gave solid weight to their opinions. After a time the ominous words were uttered in the London parliament, "America has been lost through

---

* Thurot, who has been well named "an early Paul Jones," was the leader of this French expedition. He was an Irish exile, his family name being O'Farrell. "The honour and humanity of this brave adventurer," says Lord Mahon, "are warmly acknowledged by his enemies."

† The Volunteers were mostly Protestants, but there was in the end a substantial minority of Catholics. Paul Jones, in a memorandum of his achievements, takes credit, as one of his services to human liberty, that he constrained England to suffer the Irish Volunteers.

the Irish." The example was irresistible. A convention of Volunteer officers held in the Protestant Church at Dungannon, pronounced that no power on earth save their own King, Lords, and Commons had any right to make laws for the Irish people. And they brought the force of the whole nation in support of their contention, by declaring at the same time for the immediate emancipation of the Catholics.* In the Irish Parliament there were many men of experience and ability, and one man of genius and supreme patriotism. Henry Grattan, who had now reached his 36th year, invited Parliament itself to affirm the principle of independence proclaimed at Dungannon. Parliament assented in a delirium of enthusiasm, of which the whole nation partook. Free trade was also proclaimed, to the destruction of the sacred right of England to buy, sell, and carry for the Irish. George III. would have treated these proceedings as naked rebellion

---

*On the 15th of February, 1782, the Volunteers, assembled in arms at Dungannon, adopted the following resolutions :—

"Resolved—That the claim of any body of men, other than the King, Lords, and Commons of Ireland, to make laws to bind this kingdom, is unconstitutional, illegal, and a grievance."

"Resolved—That we hold the right of private judgment in matters of religion to be equally sacred in others as in ourselves, and therefore, as men and Irishmen—as Christians and as Protestants—we rejoice in the relaxation of the Penal Laws against our Roman Catholic fellow-subjects; and we conceive the measure to be fraught with the happiest consequences to the Union, and prosperity to the Inhabitants of Ireland."

a little earlier; but the recognition of a new Republic
beyond the Atlantic, was a lesson which penetrated even
the dense prejudice of the king; and happily at the
moment, he had Charles James Fox among his advisers.
The Lord Lieutenant was instructed to confirm the declaration of independence; but the Irish leaders to avoid future
complications required the English Parliament to become
a party to the resolution, by renouncing for ever all claim
to legislate for Ireland. The English Parliament, noting
the temper of the Volunteer army and pondering doubtless on the stripes and stars which had so lately won a
place in the heraldry of nations, accordingly resolved—
" That it is the opinion of this House that the Act of the
6th of George I., entitled 'an Act for the better securing
the dependency of Ireland upon the Crown of Great
Britain,' ought to be repealed." And effect was given to
this resolution by an Act of the British Parliament
adopted without opposition or debate. It was framed in
these specific terms:—" Be it declared and enacted by the
" King's Most Excellent Majesty, by and with the advice
" and consent of the Lords spiritual and temporal, and
" Commons, in this present Parliament assembled, and by
" the authority of the same, that the said right claimed by
" the people of Ireland, to be bound only by laws enacted
" by his Majesty and the Parliament of that Kingdom, in
" all cases whatever, and to have all actions and suits at

"law or in equity, which may be instituted in that King-
"dom, decided in his Majesty's Courts therein finally, and
"without appeal from thence, shall be, and it is hereby
"declared to be established and ascertained *for ever*, and
"shall, *at no time hereafter*, be questioned or question-
"able."

Davis has interpreted this great transaction with the insight of a poet:—

> "When Grattan rose, none dare oppose
> The claim he made for freedom;
> They knew our swords to back his words,
> Were ready did he need 'em."

The motive of the concession is generally kept in the back ground by English historians, but it carries a moral too memorable and significant to be easily forgotten. A distinguished public man, who was a witness and actor in the scene, whose personal character gives his testimony exceptional weight, who, indeed, that nothing might be wanting to the force of his evidence, was the political opponent of Fox, who advised the concession, and the intimate friend of his rival, describes the feelings under which the English Parliament granted Independence to Ireland. In the Diary of Wilberforce one may read:—

"I can remember the recognition of Irish Independence,
"and how those who had talked of it as almost treason
"made no attempt to oppose it, while, if any objection was
"suggested, there was a general hush and it was whispered,

"'They have 40,000 men in arms.' My experience of
"Parliament and of the country convinces me that when
"some alarm arises in Ireland, a war, or an insurrection,
"everything will be given up at once, without those
"securities for ourselves, or that benefit to Ireland which
"might now be provided."*

In the sixteenth and seventeenth centuries it was
Catholic soldiers and statesmen who kept alive the sentiment of nationality; this last victory was won by Protestant patriots.†

Ireland had now a free Parliament which understood
her interests, and greatly promoted her material prosperity.
But in temper and prejudice it resembled an old Parliament of the Pale; its magnates being, for the most part,
men who inherited the forfeited estates, and who lived in
mortal fear of a French invasion; and while the legislature
was, in a limited sense, national, and Ireland possessed a
separate exchequer, and in effect a separate army in the
Volunteers, its Executive was still appointed from London.
The attempt to govern a country by the unnatural combination of a national Parliament and a foreign Executive,

---

* Life of Wilberforce, by his sons. Vol. IV., page 99. Murray.
1838.

† The idea of a National Guard in France is said to have been taken
from these Irish Volunteers of 1782. The purpose of the Dublin
Volunteers was not left to the imagination; their artillery was inscribed
with the plain legend—" Free Trade or else ——."

could scarcely have prospered under any circumstance, but it became hopeless when parliament by repeated offences lost the sympathy of the people. While the country grew more democratic, moved by the example of America, and of France, where the first great Revolution had broken out, parliament grew nervous and suspicious, and guarded the privileges and the abuses of the oligarchy with jealous vigilance. It refused to strengthen itself by admitting the Catholics to representation, or even to widen its bases by giving all Protestants the franchise. The Volunteers who had inspired it with courage to assert independence, attempted by a new Convention to compel it to accept reform. But Lord Charlemont, the commander of the citizen army, a great noble and a man of thought and culture, was timorous and punctilious, and at the last moment he shrank from the experiment, and, unhappily, a feud between Grattan and Flood, which smouldered since Flood's return to opposition, had flamed into mutual wrath; and co-operation between them was no longer possible. They counterbalanced each other in the national counsels, and nothing was accomplished. The people lost confidence in the Volunteers, and the Government felt it safe to disband them.

A brilliant eccentric figure which flits across the stage during the era of Independence, was the Bishop of Derry, afterwards Earl of Bristol. A class of educated men with leisure and influence, like the clergy of the Establishment, had, naturally, furnished numerous recruits to the English interest; they also lent a few exceptional men to the Patriot party. During Swift's supremacy as a popular leader,* the English interest was managed by another churchman, Hugh Boulter, an Englishman, created Archbishop of Armagh. Boulter, who was busy, greedy, and unscrupulous, was as powerful in the Castle, as Swift was in the country. The system seems to have answered, for in the time of Lucas, the English interest was led by another Archbishop of Armagh, George Stone, long the most powerful person in the kingdom; but if we may take his character from contemporary satire, a man fitter to be a freedman of Heliogabulus than a Christian prelate. And now the Bishop of Derry, though also an Englishman, competed, for a time, with Flood and Grattan, for the lead of the Volunteers, till he got eclipsed by figures of more solidity and strength. The ecclesiastics of the other Church still existed on sufferance in their native country, and could take no public part in politics; but the cause of Celtic Ireland from the flight of James to the death of

---

* Among Swift's closest allies was a brother clergyman, Dr. Sheridan, from whom so many gifted Irish men and Irish women have descended. Like Swift, he was supposed to be unfriendly to the House of Hanover, and lost a living for having taken for his text, on the birthday of George I., "Sufficient for the day is the evil thereof."

the last Stuart, found its most devoted agents among exiled priests sheltering in foreign colleges and monasteries, who served and loved it, as it was only served and loved elsewhere in that day under the tents of the Irish Brigade.

England's conquests have been won by the courage of her soldiers, not by the wisdom of her statesmen; their forecasting policy has seldom been rewarded with success. The cities which James Stuart planted as fortresses in Ulster, shut their gates, as we have seen, on his namesake and grandson. The Protestants, recruited in Germany to form a counterpoise to the French Catholics in Canada, helped to drive England out of America, while the Catholics of French descent (who in the end were shamefully treated) refused to join the movement. And now the heirs of the Scotch Settlers, regarded as a perpetual garrison for England, kindled the revolutionary spirit anew. The Northern reformers, aided by some of the Presbyterian clergy, determined to bring decisive pressure on the sluggish Parliament, and a political organisation, with the significant title of the United Irishmen, was founded at Belfast. Wolfe Tone, a young Protestant barrister of great determination of character, and endowed with winning manners and a remarkable faculty for organisation, was the founder of this society; he extended it to Dublin and managed to bring the leading Catholics of the metropolis into connection with it. His ideal was, as the title indicates, a union of the whole Irish people without local or religious distinction. A Catholic association, maintained chiefly by Dublin traders, and led by John Keogh, a merchant, who matched the Hancocks and Carrolls of the new world in brains and courage, exercised influence throughout the island; and Keogh was the friend and confederate of Tone.

The task which Tone undertook was not only a noble but an urgently needful one. The Parliament, which had asserted its independence as against England, was still an instrument of the aristocracy as servile as any of its predecessors had been to the crown. One peer controlled a dozen, another over twenty votes in the commons; and every borough had its patron. The Executive sent a crowd of placemen to College Green, whose policy they dictated. The Catholics, constituting the overwhelming bulk of the nation, had not a single member. And Flood, and many of its conspicuous men, desired to maintain this system of exclusion for ever.* The House of Lords consisted in a considerable degree of Englishmen having Irish titles conferred for some sinister service, or

---

* Goldsmith doubtless remembered the ideas of public liberty which prevailed in Dublin when he wrote—

"When I behold a factious band agree
To call it freedom when themselves are free."

of the heirs of Englishmen who had been officials in Dublin when the title was granted, and of the Bishops of the Established Church, often sent to Dublin to make a fortune as undisguisedly as adventurers in a later day were sent to Calcutta for the same purpose. The best employments in the State were held by Englishmen, some of whom had never seen the Hill of Howth; the Undertakers had to content themselves with offices which, needing personal service, were incompatible with daily attendance at the levee of Ministers, or the division lobby. The royal privilege of granting pensions was not then limited by law, and mistresses of James and William, of George I. and George II. had quartered their heirs on the Irish Establishment in company with men who earned the royal bounty by political services of a kindred character; and with kinsmen of Ministers and poor relations of the King. In pensions, salaries, and jobs English absentees drew more than a million annually out of the country. In rent they drew several millions. The corruption which appals the modern traveller in Russia, where an official cannot obtain promotion or a suitor justice, except by favoritism or bribery, where the Government is robbed by its officers, and the nation by the Government, found a parallel in Ireland ruled by a garrison of greedy place-men, and greedier place beggars. English rule in Ireland in the eighteenth century is

painted by Grattan, who knew it to the core, in a phrase
which teaches us more than volumes written on the subject
in our own day. "It could not be worse," he said, "if
they went to Hell for their principles, and to Bedlam for
men to administer them." The gentry were gay, gallant,
enjoying Patricians, who had a pride in the free parliament which they ruled, but a fear, and often a detestation,
of the people. There is not a crime recorded in Irish
history which was not represented by a great estate or a
great position. The brutal soldier, who had murdered and
plundered a territory, the scheming courtier, who gave
sly counsel how to circumvent the natives, was represented
by a noble; the untrustworthy servant who sold his
master's blood, or the convenient Judas who was a spy on
his neighbours for the officials in Dublin, by a substantial
squire; and they could neither forget their origin, nor
escape its consequences. Ireland, in that day, was like
a slave ship; a jolly crew held a carouse in the cabin,
while a multitude of their fellow creatures were starved
and stifled in the hold.

The condition of the native race contrasted with the
patriotic harangues in Parliament, as the slavery of South
Carolina or Alabama, in our day, contrasted with the
Republican fervour at Washington. They were still
excluded from both Houses, and even from the roll of
electors by whom the House of Commons was chosen;

from all the offices of the Law, the Bar, the Bench, the Grand
Jury, and the Shrievalty; from the council which managed
the affairs of their town, as much as from the council which
managed the affairs of the nation. The funds under the
control of the corporations and other civic boards were
gormandised and wasted, but as the Catholics contributed
the bulk of them it was considered an evidence of luke-
warm loyalty to ask for their audit or publication.*
Catholics were required to pay a special tax called
"quarterage," to be spent on flags and banners, feasts, and
processions to celebrate Protestant Ascendancy; they were
compelled to make good the depredations committed by
robbers in the counties in which they resided.† In the
only schools supported by the State the teaching was
exclusively Protestant; in the Charter Schools the pupils
were fed, clothed, and taught a trade, but on condition of
being, or becoming, Protestants. The children of Catholic

---

* Mr. Torrens' *Life of Lord Melbourne*, Vol. I., p. 238.

† Charles Bushe, afterwards Lord Chief Justice, instanced a transaction which happened within his own knowledge, in the county of Kilkenny. A number of villains, under the denomination of White Boys,
committed various robberies, and the grand jury, on the affidavits of the
sufferers, granted a presentment and the money was levied off the
Catholics. A short time afterwards one of the offenders was apprehended,
who proved to be a Protestant, and was executed for the offence.
Bushe said that no other proof was required to obtain a presentment on
the Roman Catholic inhabitants, than to swear that the plunderers spoke
with an Irish accent.

soldiers, the children of unknown parents in the foundling hospitals, got the same training in what was called the religion of the State as distinguished from the religion of the nation.* "The depression of the Catholics," in the language of Burke, "was not the persecution of a sect, but tyranny over a people.† But the national character had outlived persecution and corruption; and we know, on the authority of Grattan, that in the struggle for Independence " the Catholics poured in subscriptions for the service of their country, or pushed into the ranks of her glorious Volunteers." The principles of the Dungannon Convention, as far as they were designed to increase its own authority, found an echo in Parliament; but for the complete recognition of religious equality which they proclaimed, were substituted measures the very title of which read like new penal laws. An Act was

---

* This system ended by causing ignorance to be esteemed an evidence of piety and fidelity. I remember when a boy a dispute between two women, whether America belonged to England. Well," replied the one who felt herself worsted by the more strict knowledge of her antagonist, "well, dear, maybe you're right, you ought to know; but, God be thanked, I was never at a Charter School."

† Burke taught in vain how "if the Catholics were seduced or bullied from the only religion they have or can have, they must fall into indifference or into actual atheism, or its concomitant direct tendency, actual rebellion." Mr. Froude considers the chief mistake England committed was not to do more effectually what Burke denounced as madness and folly. English statesmen have to choose between these guides.

passed "to allow Persons professing the Popish Religion to teach School in this Kingdom, and for the regulating the Education of Papists, and also to repeal Parts of certain Laws relative to the Guardianship of their Children." Another which enabled Catholics to take, hold, and dispose of lands and hereditaments in the same manner as Protestants, excluded not only advowsons (which cannot be considered unreasonable, as they ought not to be permitted to nominate ministers to the Protestant Church) but manors, or boroughs returning members for Parliament, lest a chance Catholic should possess the power of selecting a Protestant member. It was ten years after the Declaration of Independence, and only when the French Republic had alarmed the English minister, that they were admitted to vote at elections.*

In following the rapid current of political history, it

---

*Pitt, who made this concession, proposed to admit them to larger liberties, but the officials in Dublin Castle were no more prepared to second his views than their predecessors had been to support the pacific policy of the Norman Kings. Grattan writing to Fox describes the result in language which we must receive with reverence, for it is stamped with the authority of the greatest living witness of the transactions. "Mr. Pitt lost the benefit of the Catholic Bill, because after he had given the law to the Catholic, he gave the execution of the law and the Catholics to their enemies. That bill had hardly appeared when the leading Minister of Ireland pronounced it an act of *insanity*, and formed an intrigue with the Ascendency Party to exclude the Catholic from getting corporate freedom, to which by that bill he was qualified. The Irish Government Press accompanied laws of reconciliation by volumes

was not possible to cast more than an occasional glance at the social and industrial condition of the country. At every stage its productive industry was sacrificed to the interest of England, with a greed that was shameless and cynical. The merchant, the manufacturer, and the farmer fell in turn under the same overshadowing and fatal influence. The landowners long suffered kindred wrongs, but they endured them with patience, because they could only keep their estates by the assistance of England. In general they compensated themselves by a constant neglect of the duties of their position. The only task they performed with punctuality was to draw inordinate rents from a famishing people; and, in process of time, a class of intermediaries, known as Middlemen, relieved them from the personal vexations of rack-renting, in return for the power of squeezing the very marrow from the bones of the people. But inordinate rents were not so destructive a wrong as a tenancy at will. We have seen how Irish cattle, living or dead, was excluded from the English market. More than half a century later, however, a cattle plague which broke out on the Continent and spread to England, made Irish beef necessary to the comfort of Englishmen, and its importation ceased to be a nuisance. The Irish landowners and Middlemen took immediately

---

of abuse against the parties to be reconciled."—Letter from Henry Grattan to Chas. Jas. Fox. Dec. 12, 1803-4.

to rearing flocks and herds; the victualing of the navy
fell into their hands; and a successful industry was speedily
established. It was conducted with inhuman indifference
to the interests of the tenants at will. Crowds of farmers
were ejected in order to throw their lands into pasture;
public commons, on which the poor had been accustomed
to feed their milch cows, were enclosed; there was no
longer employment for agricultural labourers, and there
was no Poor Law as in England. Discontent and dismay
necessarily arose; for want of land and want of wages
meant death by starvation. On the wide earth they had
neither help nor hope except in themselves, and an
agrarian conspiracy sprung up, and spread over a great
part of Leinster and Munster. Men, who wore shirts over
their ordinary dress, and from this disguise came to be
known as Whiteboys, assembled at night, pulled down the
enclosures of commons, broke up pastures, destroyed
cattle, and committed other outrages. The landlords, in order to alarm England, declared that they
were rebels aiming to bring in the Pretender, whose very
name was probably unknown to them. Cruel measures of
repression were taken against them, but they were contending for the right to live upon land which had once
been the property of their forefathers, and the conspiracy
proved to be one impossible to extirpate. Arthur Young
who thought ill of the absentees, thought still worse of the

resident proprietors in general, "the vermin of this Kingdom," he calls them, "who are never out of it, bear very heavy on the poor people, and subject them to situations more mortifying than we ever behold in England."

The Presbyterian farmers of the North were still less inclined to be patient under injustice than the Catholics of Munster, being less accustomed to its depressing discipline; they too formed an agrarian conspiracy under the title of Oak Boys, and committed the same outrages with which the Whiteboys avenged their wrongs in the South.* It cannot be disputed that North and South the people were enduring injustice to which it would have been criminal to submit. A Lord Lieutenant at this era, writing confidentially to his colleagues in London, declared that "from the rapaciousness of their unfeeling landlords, and the restrictions on their trade, they were among the most wretched people on earth."† And Bishop Berkeley, whose

---

* "In 1764, parties of the poorer Presbyterian tenants collected under the name of Oak Boys to bring landlords into more moderate dealing with them. Cattle were houghed or slashed. Farmsteads were burnt. Combinations were formed to resist cess and rent, and tithe."—Froude's *English in Ireland*.

† Lord Clonmell, Lord Chief Justice, and a thorough partisan of the English interest in parliament, has left behind him in a private diary lately published by Mr. W. J. FitzPatrick,* his impressions of the gentry, and of the Government of that era. "The Irish Government
  * *Ireland before the Union*. Dublin, 1868.

heart was moved by the sights he saw daily, demanded,
" Could any foreigner imagine that in a country, from one
port of which 107,161 barrels of beef, 7,379 barrels of
pork, and 85,729 firkins of butter are annually exported,
half the population is starving?

The state of the Agricultural classes resembled the condition of rural France before the Revolution. The farmers held at the pleasure of their landlords, and on such a tenure systematic industry is impossible. They were worse clad and fed than American slaves. The labourers lived in a condition for which there is no parallel in civilized countries. Their houses are described as being built like birds' nests, of clay, wrought together with a few sticks and some straw, and, like the nests, needing to be renewed once a year. And close at hand the great proprietors lived in a profusion nearly as ostentatious and profligate as the luxury of the French Châteaux. Famines were periodic, and came to be regarded by all but the victims with the indifference which familiarity begets. Twenty years before the Declaration of Independence there had been a peasant rising, and ten years before it, another on a larger scale,

---

resembles extremely the state of the Hottentots in Africa. The common Irish, divided, depressed, pillaged, abused as they are, are the Hottentots; the English administration are the Dutch planters; the followers of the Lord Lieutenant are the bushmen or spies and swindlers; and their wild beasts, lions, tigers, &c., *are the Irish convoys.*"

which alarmists described as a rebellion, and which was, in truth, only a struggle for life.*

The Land Law was a code, as a modern judge has declared, giving constantly increased powers to the landlords, and in which the interest of the tenant was never taken into consideration. One provision deserves to be specified as worthy of the senate in the popular fable where the sheep chose the wolves to be their legislators. Irish estates had been originally granted in return for military services claimed by the Crown, but military services were no longer required or performed, and the lands granted to the early adventurers were enjoyed without rendering any equivalent to the state or the community. After the Reformation, the estates granted were charged with the support of the Established Church, but this new duty was evaded as effectually as the old one. When the best soil was turned into pasture, and only odds and ends of inferior land left to be tilled by the natives, the Parliament in

---

* In one of these agrarian wars Spanish coins were found on some of the insurgents; a clear evidence it was assumed of their connection with foreign intriguers. The circumstance has been accounted for by the clandestine trade, maintained with Spain, in Irish wool; but, however it is to be accounted for, it will scarcely be accepted as conclusive evidence of conspiracy by readers who remember that some of the Communists killed behind the barricades of Paris, in September, 1848 (in an émeute which destroyed the Republic), had, as the English Ambassador in Paris admits, British sovereigns in their pockets !*

* Lord Normanby's *Fear of Revolutions*

Dublin was pleased to free pasture land from tithe, and ordered that import to be levied exclusively on farmers. The pastures were in the hands of land owners and Middlemen who professed the religion, and enjoyed the ministration of the Church supported by tithe; of the farmers, five-sixths were Catholics or Presbyterians.

The criminal code was harsh and brutal. "Open the statute book," said an Irish lawyer of that day, "at the word Ireland, or the word penalty, 'tis equal which, for you can trace Ireland through the statute book as you follow a wounded man through a crowd, by blood." A fair trial for a Catholic charged with a political offence was unknown; that such a person should presume to offer any defence was regarded as evidence of a stubborn spirit, and any one who abetted him was suspected of disloyalty. A priest who lectured a woman, living in open sin, for presenting herself in flaunting dress before the altar, was horsewhipped by her patron, an Irish peer, and the priest could only find at the bar of his circuit one obscure junior* bold enough to prosecute his assailant. A man charged with an offence against the Crown was not permitted by the law of England, at that time, to be defended

---

* John Philpot Curran. Thomas Russell, an officer of the British army (afterwards the confederate of Wolfe Tone), threw up the Commission of the Peace because, as he said, he could not endure to sit on a bench where it was the custom to ascertain a man's religion before inquiring into the crime with which he was charged.

by counsel, and in Ireland the "Crown" was the official title for some of the most greedy, depraved, and unscrupulous of mankind. Witnesses, indeed, might be cross-examined on his behalf, if there was money to fee a barrister. But who dare furnish money for such a purpose? To collect or contribute to a defence fund was regarded, in the precincts of Dublin Castle, as an offence amounting to abetting the crime of which the prisoner was charged. An Anglo-Irish historian complains that two Irish brothers, resident in England, and, as their mother was a Catholic, naturally suspected of treason, contributed funds for the defence of certain imprisoned Whiteboys; persons who, as the historian remarks, "were exclusively Papists," and manifestly not entitled to a fair trial. The most frigid Irish heart will swell with pride to remember that one of these Irish exiles, who had not lost interest in their poor countrymen, is known to posterity as Edmund Burke.

That a people so governed should be discontented was inevitable. But discontent extended to the whole nation excepting two favoured classes—the possessors of forfeited land, and the ministers of the Established Church, with their respective dependents. The Presbyterians, robbed of their share in the Williamite Revolution, shut out of the high places, and baffled and humiliated by the Government, were riper for resistance than the Catholics, and many Church of England men shared their discontent, for

they too had been robbed in the interest of England.
From the time of William their manufactures and commerce had been continuously depressed to appease English
rivalry. Every article manufactured in England could be
carried into Ireland, no article manufactured in Ireland
could be carried into England. Ireland could not trade
directly with any of the British colonies, or any of the
British colonies with Ireland. Rum from Jamaica, or
timber from Canada must be landed in an English port,
and re-shipped, before it could be offered to Irish customers.
The Irish Parliament had now proclaimed Free Trade, and
was making deliberate efforts to recover manufactures, but
the process of reviving a ruined industry is a slow one.

The treatment of the Presbyterians had produced its
natural fruit. The merchants and traders of Scotch
descent, especially in Belfast, and the more educated and
thoughtful of the farmers and shopkeepers of the same
race throughout the Northern provinces, were democrats.
They had sympathised with the resistance of the American
Colonies, and with the French Revolution, and many of
them with the claims of the Catholics to religious liberty.
Their share of political power, however, was slight; in their
chief stronghold, Belfast, they had no more control over the
election of the members than the Papists; the patron of the
borough, Lord Donegal, relieving them of that responsibility.
The landowners whether Scotch or English, who feared

that any change would endanger their inordinate authority, were mostly of the party of resistance, and were vehement supporters of Protestant Ascendancy, because Protestant Ascendancy ensured them a following among the lower classes, on the same easy terms that Negro slavery in a later day gave the planters in the Southern States of America, a following among the Mean Whites. They took pains to promote a sectarian spirit among the Protestant peasantry, as a counterpoise to the democracy of the towns; and their teaching produced tragic excesses a little before the period we have now reached, upon which it is necessary to pause.

Armagh was one of the most prosperous of the counties planted under James I. The population, which consisted mainly of Protestants of English descent, had increased at the ratio which prosperity ensures, and they began to feel the want of more space. Some of the original population held farms, which by their industry had become worth coveting, and it was resolved to get possession of them. A secret society was formed for this purpose, called the Peep-o'-Day Boys; and for a period of between two and three years it held wide districts under the same brute authority which Lord George Gordon's mob exercised in London a few years earlier. Grattan described them as " a banditti of murderers committing massacre in the name of God, and exercising despotic power in the name of liberty." Their mode of proceeding was simple and expeditious. Armed gangs assembled between midnight and early morning, and gave notice at every Catholic house in a district that the inhabitants must be off to Connaught or Hell at their option, by an appointed day, or written notice of banishment was posted on their doors. If they did not fly before the day named, the gang returned, drove them out, sometimes in the bitter nights of an Irish winter, wrecked their houses, and destroyed all their moveable property; their immovable property was divided a little later, among the conspirators and their friends. There was no redress. The local magistrates were secret confederates of the mob; and the Executive in Dublin looked on with indifference or complacency. Before any effectual check was put on these proceedings it is estimated that six thousand Catholics were banished and had all their property confiscated. They naturally attempted some resistance; a rude organization was formed, named the Defenders, a title which speaks for itself. But it was nearly as dangerous to succeed as to fail; their persecutors could scarcely deal harder with them than the law, administered by Peep-o'-Day magistrates, was sure to do if they presumed to defend themselves. Lord Gosford, the Lieutenant of the County, had not only derived his estate from confiscation, and held it, as he said himself, by a "Protestant title," but was a confirmed supporter of

Protestant Ascendancy in Church and State. He was a
man of justice and humanity, however, and he could not
look on in silence at this iniquity. Early in the movement
he called together the grand panel of the county, and
exhorted them to form a committee of gentlemen holding
the commission of the peace to arrest further violence, and
bring offenders to justice. He did not accomplish much
as an arbiter, but he has left on record contemporary
evidence of the utmost value; the testimony of the highest
official in the county, uttered at a meeting of his neighbours who could call him to account for any error or
exaggeration.

"It is no secret," he said, "that a persecution, accompanied with
"circumstances of ferocious cruelty, which have in all ages
"distinguished that dreadful calamity, is now raging in this
"county. Neither age nor sex, or even acknowledged innocence
"as to any guilt in the late disturbance, is sufficient to excite
"mercy, much less to afford protection. The only crime which the
"wretched objects of this ruthless persecution are charged with, is
"a crime, indeed, of easy proof; it is simply a profession of the
"Roman Catholic faith, or an intimate connexion with a person
"professing this faith. A lawless banditti have constituted
"themselves judges of this new species of delinquency, and the
"sentence they have denounced is equally concise and terrible.
"It is nothing less than a confiscation of all property, and an
"immediate banishment. It would be extremely painful, and
"surely unnecessary, to detail the horrors that attend the execution
"of so rude and tremendous a proscription,—a proscription that
"certainly exceeds, in the comparative number of those it consigns
"to ruin and misery, every example that ancient and modern

"history can supply: for where have we heard, or in what story "of human cruelties have we read, of more than half the inhabi- "tants of a populous country deprived at one blow of the means "as well as of the fruits of their industry, and driven, in the "midst of an inclement season, to seek a shelter for themselves "and their helpless families where chance may guide them. This "is no exaggerated picture of the horrid scenes now acting in this "county. Yet surely it is sufficient to awaken sentiments of "indignation and compassion in the coldest bosom. These "horrors are now acting with impunity. The spirit of im- "partial justice (without which law is nothing better than an "instrument of tyranny), has for a time disappeared in this "county, and the supineness of the magistracy of Armagh is "become a common topic of conversation in every corner of the "Kingdom."

These horrors might be forgotten if they had not bequeathed us a permanent legacy. But out of the Peep-o'-Day Boys sprang, in the end, the Orange Society; an organization which the landlords of Ulster have used for nearly a century in guarding their class interests; "getting," in the language of an eminent Orangeman, "all they could in the name of Protestantism, and sacrificing without scruple all that their poorer Protestant brethren venerated."*

---

* We have paused at times in this rapid survey to note how Irish History is presented to English readers, and in what a painful relation names eminent and cherished in England sometimes associate themselves with Irish affairs. These Armagh outrages furnish another curious illustration of both circumstances. Coleridge is a name dear to the cultivated class in all communities where the English tongue is spoken,

To reform such a parliament, to amend such laws, to
purge such a magistracy were tasks of true statesmanship, and they constituted the original design of the
United Irishmen. But the parliament would not consent
to be reformed, and the amendments of the law which it
accepted were pitifully inadequate. The Catholics were

---

and it is still represented in the liberal professions by eminent and
honoured men. In the current edition of the Works of Samuel Taylor
Coleridge (read by the bulk of thoughtful English students) the story of
the Peep-o'-Day Boys is told, but told with a difference. The *dramatis
personæ* are transposed ; the unhappy Catholics, who were expelled and
robbed, are described as the Peep-o'-Day Boys, and their triumphant
persecutors as the Defenders! The extract is worth printing for the
benefit of English publicists of our own day who make Irish affairs a
study. "Is all history a dream? I involuntarily repeat, or is it not
even beyond historic faith more certain that in the winter 1791-1792, a
multitude of the lower Papists leagued together with the express design
of rooting out Protestants and Protestantism from the county of Armagh.
. . . In the horror of individual atrocities, in the exclusive choice
and selection of the victims, in all but opportunity and consequent extent, might not the Armagh outrages be identified with the murder of
the two hundred thousand Protestants in the reign of the unhappy
Charles? . . . It was but a few days prior to the outburst of these
'Peep-o'-Day Boys' in the Northern counties that the candidates for
power and popularity had begun to use the supposed wrongs of the
Romanists. . . . Abandoned to their own resources, replaced, as it
were, under the government of nature, and remitted to her imprescriptible laws of self preservation and self defence, harassed from hour to
hour, taught by experience that neither sex, nor infancy, nor sleep, was
deemed sacred by their leagued and sworn assassins, the afflicted Protestants were at length compelled to form a counter-league, and under
the just appellation of Defenders, associating in armed bodies, soon re-

permitted to become barristers, but prohibited from being judges, and from enjoying any of the prizes of their profession. They were admitted to the franchise, but still shut out from the corporations and parliament; and it must be confessed that voting for somebody else to enjoy an office from which you are excluded is a somewhat barren pleasure.

A Lord Lieutenant was sent over who desired to treat the bulk of the nation fairly, but he was required to perform the impossible task of carrying out his policy through agents to whom it was odious. The British peers, with Irish estates, were alarmed by the clamour of the Undertakers in Dublin, and the experiment was hastily abandoned. English critics at that period expressed the same sagacious wonder which we have witnessed in our own time, that the Catholics were not content and thankful with this contemptible fragment of their rights;

---

pelled and suppressed their enemies."* Coleridge, no doubt, mistold the story, not through malice but through ignorance and carelessness, but how many thousand English readers have since accepted his version as authentic? As he repeats the fables and exaggerations of 1641 as if they were gospel, so other writers, on his authority, will tell this story of Catholic persecution, and Protestant suffering to new generations of Englishmen. Mr. Froude, in his *English in Ireland*, has an account of the origin of the Peep-o'-Day Boys, less egregiously, but quite as intrinsically, fabulous as the metamorphosis accomplished by Coleridge.

* Coleridge's Essays on his own Times, Vol. III.; p. 717.—London : Pickering. 1850.

as if men are ever content with being cheated; but the Lord Lieutenant warned the Prime Minister in private, that half measures must necessarily produce dissatisfaction, " to make a reservation," he said, " is to leave a splinter in the wound."*

Grattan and his friends brought on the Catholic question, and the Pension List anew, and aimed again and again to widen the basis of parliament, and to purify it from influences under which it was perishing. He directly charged Ministers with selling the favour of the Crown for money to be spent in corruption; and moved for a committee to inquire whether they had not created peers in consideration of funds spent to secure the election of government candidates. But always in vain; the chief

---

* Lord Fitzwilliam to the Duke of Portland. There is a vague impression among Englishmen that the enactment of Penal Laws ceased with the coming in of the House of Hanover; but this impression is far from being accurate; it ceased with the battle of Fontenoy; the old laws began to be relaxed after the battle of Gemappe. As late as the beginning of the eighteenth century, when George I. was king, the Privy Council in Dublin, two Bishops participating in the transaction, sent the heads of a Bill to England, which provided that every unregistered priest or friar found in the country after the eighteenth of May, 1720, shall have a large P branded on his cheek with hot irons. But they did not think this measure adequate, and amended it by a further provision, that he should be subject to an outrage which can be only indicated; the same which the Grand Turk inflicts on the guardians of his seraglio. The English Privy Council, however, declined to sanction the project, and it had to be abandoned.

function of the Lord Lieutenant in that day, indeed, was to procure by profuse favours and promises, a majority which would prevent the Irish Parliament from becoming indestructible by planting its foundations in the confidence of the whole nation. For already Pitt, who was now Minister, was preparing from afar off the project of a Union.

The French Revolution, which in those days seemed destined to conduct mankind to happier and nobler regions of existence, rendered the United Irishmen impatient of delay and weary of appeals to a stubborn oligarchy. They transformed their society into a secret conspiracy to break the connection with England, and establish an Irish Republic.* The society had now at its head a young soldier sprung from a great historic house, and closely allied with great English houses. Lord Edward Fitzgerald was son of the Duke of Leinster, nephew of the Duke of Richmond, and cousin-german of Charles James Fox. He was of an eminently handsome presence, derived from a mother who was one of the noted beauties of her day, and of winning manners. Though he inherited the blood

---

* "What is our end? The rights of man in Ireland! The greatest happiness of the greatest numbers in this island; the inherent and indefeasible claims of every free nation to rest in this nation; the will and power to be happy; to pursue the common weal as an individual pursues his private welfare, and to stand in insulated independence an imperatorial people."—*Plan of the United Irish Society.*

of the Stuarts, and the better blood of the Geraldines, and
was reared in a palace, he embraced ardently the principles
of popular liberty taught by Mirabeau. Among the
Directory of the United Irish Society the most conspicuous
men were Arthur O'Connor, nephew to Lord Longueville,
Thomas Addis Emmet, a barrister of distinguished ability,
Samuel Neilson, a Belfast trader and Editor of the
Northern Star, Henry and John Sheares, sons of a Cork
banker, Dr. Mac Nevin, heir of one of the Irish families
banished to Connaught by Cromwell, and many other
young men of good family, or good professional position.
The man of genius who had founded the society was
obliged to fly the country, and was in Paris soliciting aid
from the French Republic. Though the design was to
establish a democracy, the society counted among its allies
and sympathisers, the heirs of several peers and commoners
of large property.* Grattan, Curran, and the leaders of
the national party in Parliament held aloof, but Parliament by its obduracy had so disappointed them that they
did not withhold their sympathy. The Government afterwards strove to connect Grattan with the conspiracy, but
failed; Curran was less cautious. Charles Hamilton
Teeling, in his venerable age, told me that in '97, when he

---

* Lord Lauderdale was said to be among its English allies. Lord
Byron, half a generation later, wrote in his Diary, "If I had been a
man. I should have made an English Lord Edward Fitzgerald."

was a United Irishman and a young leader of the Ulster Catholics, Curran meeting him in College Green, took him under the colonnade of the Parliament House, and whispered reproachfully, "When will you begin, *when will you begin?*"

Keogh, the leader of the Catholics, was not averse to the designs of the United Irishmen. He was cautious as beseemed the guardian of a defeated cause, but he was in communication with Tone (who indeed was secretary to the Catholic Committee), and it was well understood that any rational attempt for liberty would have his active aid. What the Catholics could furnish to the enterprise was fighting men, and a few middle-class leaders. The remnant of their nobility and gentry were more alarmed at revolution than the Government itself; and the clergy, who had barely a legal existence, were in general only anxious to perform their duties without attracting notice. A returned exile occasionally reminded them of what they had once been. Lord Taaffe, who had served with distinction in Austria, both as a soldier and diplomatist, visited Ireland during the era of independence. The minister of Austria, who was naturally received as an equal by the ministers of England, saw with shame and scorn his countrymen disciplined to regard themselves as an inferior race, because they professed the faith whose servants he was accustomed to see occupy the foremost place in Courts and Councils of State. The feelings which this strange spectacle begot in a Count of the Holy Roman Empire, he strove, not entirely without success, to communicate to his own order, and to the growing middle class in Dublin. Lord Trimblestone, another Catholic peer, reared in the Court of Versailles and driven home by the French Revolution, succeeded Lord Taaffe as temporary leader or spokesman of the Catholics. But he was strangely out of unison with the spirit of the epoch. While Europe was shaken by the new doctrines proclaimed from the ruins of the Bastile, and the Catholics were dreaming of complete religious and national freedom, he is described by a competent critic,* as exhibiting the demeanour and holding the principles of an *émigré* of the army of Condé. Had the Catholics needed any goad except their wrongs to stimulate them to revolution, parliament, since their complaints had become troublesome, passed a Convention Act, to prevent them pursuing a peaceful agitation effectually. And they were able doubtless to read the moral of the American Revolution; the colonies which had fought for liberty had obtained it; Catholic Canada, the only colony which had refused to fight against the Crown, still remained, and, indeed, remained for two generations more, under the most galling misgovernment.

---

* Wyse's History of the "Catholic Association."

The story of the insurrection of '98 would swell to a volume, and we are only permitted a hasty glance. In anticipation of the struggle the Government embodied a militia of thirty thousand men, consisting in great part of recruits whom Orange magistrates recommended as free from the taint of patriotism. They did not prove quite free, however, for it became necessary to make examples among them, and four of the Monaghan militia were shot for sympathy with the national cause. Suspected Irish regiments were exchanged for regiments from Scotland or Wales, and the regular army was greatly strengthened, till nearly a hundred thousand soldiers were accumulated in the island. The United Irish Society had more than twice as many enrolled members. When the plans of the leaders were nearly ripe for action a colonel in the insurgent army sold his associates to the government. This was Thomas Reynolds. Originally a Catholic country gentleman, and brother-in-law to the incorruptible founder of the Society, he had silently abandoned his religion and his principles for opinions more profitable and convenient. On this information, Lord Edward was arrested, after having received a mortal wound; the other principal leaders also fell into the hands of the Government, and the insurrection hung fire. A rising in Ulster, where a handful of Presbyterian and Catholic farmers fought two battles with the King's troops, was speedily suppressed. A French invasion was still expected however; it was rumoured that young General Buonaparte, or young General Hoche, who was more highly esteemed at that period, would lead it, and it became the policy of the Government to compel the disaffection to explode in the South also before foreign assistance could arrive.

In the County Wexford the United Irishmen had enrolled few recruits, but the Government devised a method of manufacturing rebels which would have tortured a settlement of Quakers into resistance. The County was delivered over to a militia, who were permitted, and encouraged, to live at free quarters. These soldiers, who were chiefly loyalists from an English plantation in Cork, invented a number of devices which were considered very pleasant and ingenious by the friends of Government. The French Republicans had set the example of close cropped hair, and if any Wexford peasant was discovered whose hair was not of an orthodox length he was dragged into a Barracks, and a cap of coarse linen, smeared with pitch, pulled over his head; when the pitch had properly hardened he was turned out to a loyal mob, who amused themselves in tearing off the cap, and as patches of the hair and scalp came with every tug, the amusement was exhilarating. But the supply of "Croppies," was limited, and it was considered good sport to manufacture them.

Suspected persons had their hair forcibly trimmed to the republican model, and the jovial operators sometimes heightened the fun by clipping the ears as well as the hair. To vary the pleasure moist powder was smeared over the crop, and it was set on fire, and the Croppy allowed to run home hunted by a loyal pack of pursuers. Sometimes suspected persons were half hanged to extort confessions against their neighbours, sometimes they were flogged to the point of death for the same purpose. Sometimes they were picketed; that is to say suspended by the arms, while the only resting place for the foot was a pointed stake. If a peasant could not be found when these sportsmen wanted him his house was burned. They next betook themselves to burning Catholic chapels; for it is very essential in relation to events which followed that the reader should understand that the peasants were Catholics, and their torturers invariably Protestants. The number of chapels destroyed before the people resisted has not been ascertained with certainty, but before and after that event, nearly sixty Catholic chapels were sacked and burned by soldiers and yeomen. At length the people felt it was better to die as their ancestors had died, than live in this hell upon earth. The resistance was begun by Father John Murphy, a priest educated on the Continent, and living in the peaceful performance of his duties as long as peace was possible.

But his chapel having been burned down, he called out his congregation, and took the field. Other priests followed his example, and they swept the British troops out of every stronghold in the county. The whole Catholic population rose, placed at their head Protestant squires of patriotic sentiment, but no military training, and organised an insurrectionary camp and army. The young farmers who acted as their aides-de-camp, however, proved so fit for their work that some of them afterwards rose to distinction in the service of Napoleon.*

Had a fourth of Ireland followed the example of Wexford, there would probably have been a revolution. But the Wexford men were unsupported, and after a campaign like that which was fought for the Bourbons in La Vendée, were finally defeated. A little later a French expedition procured, and accompanied by Wolfe Tone, landed in the West, but it was too feeble in number for its purpose, and it arrived when the contest was at an end. The Government hanged Presbyterian ministers in the North, and Catholic priests in the South; then came the courts-martial, and the savage excesses of troops taught to regard the campaign as a religious war. For the gentry had appealed to the fear of Popery, which it is never difficult to awaken in men of British descent, and the

---

* See "Memoirs of Miles Byrne, Chef de Bataillon, Officer of the Legion of Honour, etc." Paris : Gustave Bossange et Cie. 1863.

Orange Society was founded ostensibly to retain the Catholics in subjection, but really to avoid a revolution in which the estates got by the sword might be lost by the sword. The cruelties which made the name of Cumberland a sound of horror to the Scottish nation half a century before, were repeated by Carhampton in Ireland in 1798.* The Armagh regiment recruited from Orangemen, and heirs of the Peep-o'-Day Boys, and the North Cork Regiment were the most savage of the local force. But German troops, still known to the people as the Hessians, and a Welsh regiment who called themselves Ancient Britons, have left memories nearly as terrible. Suspected peasants were carried on board tenders on the mere order of a military officer, and only released on undertaking to serve in the British army or navy. Many were exchanged for German soldiers, and sent to die in foreign wars. Some, it is alleged, were sold to the Prussian Government, as Cromwell sold their forefathers to West Indian planters. No one who is not blind or besotted can deny the great qualities by which the

---

* Lord Carhampton was an Irishman; the head of a house whose representative in the army of James II. has made the family name of Luttrell a synonym for traitor in Ireland. Colonel Luttrell is said to have delivered to the enemy an important pass which he was appointed to guard at the battle of Aughrim. From this transaction has come the familiar peasant phrase for public or domestic treachery, "He sowld the pass!"

English race have won their position in the world, but they have been from the beginning, and continue down to this day, the most merciless of conquerors. These memories are painful and revolting, but who can blot them out? As long as the breast of an Englishman will glow with just pride as he reads of Creçy, or Agincourt, the Nile or Waterloo, so long the heart of an Irishman will be disturbed by agony and wrath over the desolation of Desmond, the spoliation of Ulster, and the brutalities of Carhampton.*

It is certain that the Government encouraged the formation of the Orange Society, and it was widely believed by moderate and experienced men, that they fomented the excesses in Wexford in order to divide Protestants and Catholics, and open a way for the Union. This charge has been denounced as base and groundless in our time; but at least it rests on respectable authority. "I accuse him," said Plunket, speaking of Lord Castlereagh, "of fomenting the embers of a lingering rebellion; of hallooing the

---

* "Pitt permitted in Ireland a reign of terror hardly less atrocious, though better concerted, than the massacres of September, and the fusillade at Lyons."—*Thorold Rogers.*

Writing of the execution of John and Henry Shears, (two of the United Irish Directory who were hanged in Dublin), Robert Southey, in a letter to his friend William Taylor, of Norwich, says, "The Irish business has been almost a counterpart to the death of the Girondists; yet who would not be content so to die in order so to have lived?"

Protestant against the Catholic, and the Catholic against the Protestant; of artfully keeping alive domestic dissensions for the purpose of subjugation."

In Wexford, some peasants of savage temper committed cruelties which fatally seconded the policy of the Government. They burned a barn at Scullabogue, containing nearly two hundred prisoners, the vast majority of whom were Protestants, and they avenged themselves barbarously at Wexford and Vinegar Hill, on many of their local enemies, who were of the same creed. No crimes ever committed were more fatal in their consequences, for they arrested the union of Catholic and Protestant on which the prosperity of the country depended. But they understand human nature imperfectly who think that any peasantry ever existed, who, having suffered the wanton cruelties which had driven Wexford to arms, could be restrained from avenging themselves on their torturers, whatever their creed might be.*

Parliament so far from proving a shelter to the people

---

* " According to some accounts, about fifteen Catholics perished in this barn. But I find in a letter from Dr. Caulfield to Dr. Troy, of the 29th of October, 1799, that he could mention but seven, viz.:—two men of the name of Neille, the clerk of Mr. Shalloe's chapel, Johnston, a piper, Eleanor Ryan, a servant maid, Edward Ryan, her father, and Edward Killa, a herd."—Plowden's *Historic Survey*.

These execrable crimes were denounced in a proclamation by the Irish commander, who declared "That any person or persons who should take upon him or them to kill or murder any person or prisoner, burn any

in their trouble proved a scourge. Up to the eve of the insurrection, Grattan, who was a Whig of the school of Burke, still fought the battle of religious, and of public liberty, by constitutional methods. But the house which he had liberated from servile bonds rejected his authority. A bill introduced by him to emancipate the Catholics (as completely as they were afterwards emancipated in 1829), was lost by a majority of three to one.* On an amendment to the address he could muster only fourteen supporters, and on another occasion only a dozen, in a division where a hundred and sixty members voted. In 1797 he made a final effort for parliamentary reform; was followed by only thirty members

---

house, or commit any plunder, without special written orders from the commander-in-chief should suffer death." It was afterwards proved that Catholic priests had striven to arrest the murders; that it was against Orangemen and Persecutors alone the rage of the peasantry was excited, that Protestants who had not injured them suffered no wrong in any town which fell into their hands; that the soldiers and yeomen had set the example of the wanton murder of prisoners; and that rumours of new murders following the defeat of the insurgents at Ross, had provoked the outrages at Scullabogue, but after all has been said the transaction remains a foul stain on the national cause.

* When the Anglo-Irish gentry had lost their parliament and their power, and had become the mere tail of an English party, Grattan reminded them in the House of Commons in London, that this humiliating reverse had been brought about by their own bigotry. "When the Irish Parliament rejected the Catholic Petition, on that day she voted the Union; many good and pious reasons she gave, and she lies there with her many good and her pious reas..ns."

against a hundred and seventeen, and then seceded from the House in despair. During the insurrection he was in England in dilapidated health, tortured by wrongs and sufferings which he could not avert. At this propitious time, George III. recognised his public services by striking his honoured name from the list of Privy Councillors with his own hand.

The Parliament which he had abandoned in despair, sanctioned the savage excesses of the gentry, and supported the barbarous policy of Castlereagh and Carhampton. Acts were passed protecting magistrates from the legal consequences of their recent violence, rendering it a transportable offence to return from banishment inflicted by a court-martial, imposing the penalty of high treason on certain refugees if they did not surrender in a few weeks, and confiscating the property of Lord Edward and other prominent leaders. "The poor," as Grattan said, "were struck out of the protection of the law; the rich out of its penalties." No Parliament of the Pale was a more servile instrument of torture in the hands of a Lord Deputy than this free Parliament of Anglo-Norman gentry and English placemen became in the hands of Castlereagh.* But

---

*The nature and extent of the official crimes, into which these acts forbade enquiry, are described by Lord Holland in his "History of the Whig Party."

"Trials, if they must so be called, were carried on without number

they exacted their price; when the insurrection was at an end soldiers were ordered to be still kept billetted on the people at free quarters, "till all rents, taxes, and tithes were completely paid up."

Pitt seized the opportunity of public calamity and panic to carry a measure, the bare proposal of which, half a dozen years earlier, would have endangered the British connection. By the stern suppression of opinion, and the profligate purchase of votes he carried an act establishing a legislative union between Ireland and Great Britain. Martial law still prevailed in the country, and several meetings to petition against the project, were dispersed by force. But out of a population of between three or four millions, the petitioners against the measure amounted to

---

under martial law. It often happened that three officers composed the court, and that of the three two were under age, and the third an officer of the yeomanry or militia, who had sworn in his Orange lodge eternal hatred to the people over whom he was thus constituted a judge. Floggings, picketings, death, were the usual sentences: and these were sometimes commuted into banishment, serving in the fleet, or transference to a foreign service. Many were sold at so much per head to the Prussians. . . . Dr. Dickson (Lord Bishop of Down), assured me that he had seen families returning peaceably from Mass, assailed without provocation, by drunken troops and yeomanry, and the wives and daughters exposed to every species of indignity, brutality, and outrage, from which neither his remonstrances nor those of other Protestant gentlemen could rescue them. The subsequent Indemnity Acts deprived of redress the victims of this wide-spread cruelty."

over seven hundred thousand; as large a proportion as ever spoke in behalf of any nation.

On its first proposal the motion was defeated. But a base band of Anglo-Norman and Cromwellian gentry, Bagwells and Rowleys, of whom there were three each in the House of Commons, Creightons, of whom there were two, Browne, Fortescue, Neville, Preston, Rochfort, French, and so forth, sold their votes and changed sides. Of the supporters of the measure first and last a list of a hundred and forty has been published, specifying in each case the exact price of the member's conscience. They were costly convertites these Anglo-Irish gentlemen. The agencies of corruption have been described by an orator who has made the question his own.

"Within the Parliament," says O'Connell, "a majority was bought and paid for. Over a million sterling was spent in secret bribes, and a million and a quarter openly in buying the interest, which patrons were supposed to possess in the right of boroughs to representation. In the army, in the navy, in the customs, patronage was distributed as bribes. Those who preferred money down got a sum of £8,000 for a vote, but an office of £2,000 a year was not considered too high an equivalent. No less than twenty peerages, ten bishoprics, one Chief Justiceship, and six puisne Judgeships, were given to men who voted for the Union."[*]

Beresfords and Trenches (there were three each in the Commons), Tottenhams, Packenhams, and Longfields,

---

[*] O'Connell's speech before the Corporation of Dublin.

(there were two each), Fitzgerald, Blackwood, Jocelyn, Knox, Langrishe, Westenra, and others, of what was called the best blood of the English-Irish, supported the measure from the first. And the peerages of Clanmorris, Dufferin, Ennismore, de Blacquiere, Castlecoote, Rossmore, Cloncurry, Tyrawly, Dunalley, Wallscourt, Norbury, and several more, were called into existence to reward their devotion. It had its root in corruption as profligate as any recorded in human history; and its fruit has still been racy of the evil soil from which it sprang. Pitt's most efficient agent in these transactions was an apostate as shameless, but less strong, than Strafford. Robert Stewart, who began public life by mounting a green cockade, and toasting the Rights of Man, was now, as Lord Castlereagh,* Chief Secretary and leader of the Irish Government. He was a poor debater, but otherwise well fitted for his appointed task, being nearly as resolute, adroit, and unscrupulous as the eminent statesman whom he represented.

The men who resisted the Union belonged to two classes, each of which suggests curious reflections. The first included every man who has come down to our times memorable for honourable services, Grattan, Plunket, Ponsonby, afterwards Lord Chancellor, Bushe, afterwards Lord Chief Justice, the representative of the great Celtic

---

* His father had become Marquis of Londonderry.

house of O'Brien, and of the great Celtic house of O'Donnell, and the Latouches, Parnells, and Shaws of the Anglo-Irish race. The other included the loyalists who had performed most signal services for the Crown in the late insurrection; Lord Kingsborough, colonel of the most barbarous regiment of militia, Maxwell Barry, and Lord Corry, colonels of other regiments employed in similar service, and William Saurin, the patron and leader of the Orangemen for a quarter of a century.*

In England, Burke, Fox, and Gray, opposed it. Fox declared that "the whole scheme went upon that false and abominable presumption that we could legislate better for the Irish nation than they could for themselves,—a principle founded upon the most arrogant despotism and tyranny. . . There was no maxim more true in philosophy or in politics than the great moral doctrine, "Do as you would be done by." And what Englishman

---

*The contest produced, as a great political fermentation commonly does, men of fervid imagination and passionate enthusiasm. And it trained profound constitutionalists. It is curious to note that the system of parliamentary government, as it is now administered, was apparently better understood in Ireland, as it was afterwards better understood among men of French descent in Lower Canada, than at its place of birth. Ireland had not got responsible Ministers in our sense (nor, indeed, had England), but the cardinal principles of the system of English liberty, and the consequences which flow from them, were never presented with more luminous force than in the debates on the Union.

would submit to see his destiny regulated and his affairs
conducted by persons chosen for Belfast or Limerick?
. . . We ought not to presume to legislate for a nation,
in whose feelings and affections, wants and interests,
opinions and prejudices, we have no sympathy." The
names of these statesmen have still decisive authority with
Englishmen on all questions except this cardinal one.
To mitigate the opposition of the Catholics, Pitt privately
communicated to their leaders that the British Parliament would grant them the complete Emancipation which
the Parliament in Dublin had persistently denied. Pitt,
who was not a bigot, who had allied England with the
Catholic states of the Continent against France, and who
was defending the Empire with an army in a large part
Catholic, intended to perform all he promised. But when
the time to perform came, George III. interposed the same
stupid resistance which had lost America; and Pitt yielded
his convictions and his plighted word to the fanaticism of
the imbecile King.*

---

* Another promise which heralded the Union, was that the public
employments of the empire, civil and military, should be thrown open to
Irishmen. Lord Colchester, a Tory, and a bitter opponent of Catholic
Emancipation, describes one feeble attempt to keep the promise. The
Lord Lieutenant (Lord Hardwicke), desired to obtain some military
patronage to be distributed among Irishmen, (Irish Protestants *bien
entendu*); but the Duke of York resisted, and he never obtained a single
ensigncy for any Irishman whom he recommended (1801).—Lord
Colchester's "Diary," Vol. I., p. 278.

The venality of this parliament has been a standing reproach to Ireland; and it is considered an effectual answer to her claims to govern herself that when she had the opportunity of electing a legislature, she chose one which sold her liberties without shame. The purchased parliament, which declined to reform itself, has been already described. It consisted of three hundred members, among whom were a hundred placemen, subject not to Ireland but to the British crown, and more than a hundred nominees sitting for close boroughs and close counties, the creatures of a few peers, and great proprietors. And in this parliament only a bare majority was obtained for the Union. The Catholics constituting four-fifths of the nation, were wholly unrepresented. The traffic was shameful; but those who are familiar with the career of Walpole and the Pelhams, may reasonably inquire, if corruption is to disfranchise a people for ever, whether there might not be found other nations who have forfeited their right to parliamentary institutions?

The Irish were at last—so it was proclaimed—admitted to perfect brotherhood. It is a curious phenomenon that each great change which England meditated was sweetened by a general admission of past transgressions. Sir John Davies confessed with charming frankness that up to the coming of James I. the Irish were naturally and inevitably enemies of the English Crown, from the treatment they had received. And now Pitt summed up the history of the connection in a pregnant sentence, " England," he declared, " had contrived to deprive Ireland of the use of her own revenues, and render her subservient to British interests and opulence." But the Union would set these wrongs for ever right. How far it has set them right, no one is ignorant. Thenceforth the Irish people sent representatives to the great senate of the Empire, and were in full enjoyment of British liberty ; if British liberty consists in being heard with visible impatience, and peremptorily outvoted, on every national question, by a majority who do not trouble themselves to listen to the debate. In the language of an obscure observer, this transaction " broke the heart and sucked the brains of the country." Molyneux, who first formulated the case of Ireland, lays down a proposition which is as true of this transaction, happening nearly a century after his death, as of the transaction to which he applies it. " If a villain, with a pistol at my breast, makes me convey my estate to him, no one will say that this gives him any right, and yet such a title as this has an unjust conqueror who, with a sword at my throat, forces me into submission."

After the Union Robert Emmet, the boy brother of one of the United Irish leaders, and Thomas Russell, the bosom friend of Wolfe Tone, attempted a new insurrection, but it was inadequately supported ; they fell into the hands of the British Government, and were added to the long list of martyrs for Irish liberty. This attempt is usually treated as hair-brained and hopeless, but the young enthusiast declared that men of great position and authority were parties to it; and it is certain that four months after it had failed, Napoleon Buonaparte, then First Consul, answered an appeal of Emmet's eldest brother by promising to send an expedition to Ireland at an early day.

The Catholics under John Keogh kept alive their organization and their hopes notwithstanding the duplicity of Pitt. Between the Revolution of 1688 and the American war, Protestants, however distinguished for patriotism or benevolence, had been implacable in their hostility to Catholics. Neither Swift nor Berkeley, Flood nor Charlemont proposed to extend the Irish liberty which he desired beyond the pale of the minority. Since 1782, however, a constantly increasing number of Protestants were eager to see the emancipation of the Catholics completed; but the bulk of those in possession of monopolies hated the race which put them in peril, with the merciless hatred that a tyrant still feels towards the slave who conspires for deliverance.

The credit of those who strive and suffer is commonly swallowed up in the credit of those who succeed; and the Irish Catholics are scarcely aware how much they owe to John Keogh. He organised the country so effectually that a Lord Lieutenant warned a Secretary of State, that this Dublin merchant was exercising the highest functions of Government, levying contributions which were promptly paid, and issuing orders which were cheerfully obeyed. And Edmund Burke forgot the cares of empire to exchange encouragement and counsel with the committee guided by Keogh; for the Irish cause, which is a jest to the English Philistine, exercised an irresistible fascination over the mind of Burke, as it exercised an irresistible fascination over the minds of Grattan, Sheridan and Canning. A struggle protracted through all the years of his manhood, many bitter disappointments, and probably the unconscious influence of age, at length lowered Keogh's hopes, and he recommended a policy of delay and quiescence. But the new generation, represented by a vigorous lawyer in the flush of manhood, was impatient of delay. O'Connell to his latest day was fond of describing the Catholic conference where Keogh counselled a "dignified repose," and where he, the representative of the coming time, followed, and not opposing or controverting what the venerable patriot had recommended, but treating his suggestion with infinite respect, caused an exactly opposite course to be adopted by the meeting. But a calamity, which has since befallen Ireland more than once, soon ensued; the influential and the timid retired in alarm, and there were long two jarring factions of Catholics more anxious to thwart each other than to press upon their common enemy. Among English statesmen, however, their cause gained ground, and it is probable that Emancipation might have arrived a dozen years earlier than it came, if they had not desired to accompany it with conditions to which the bulk of Irish Catholics could not assent. It was proposed to give the Crown an indirect veto on the selection of Catholic Bishops; and the Bishops chosen were required to furnish to certain Commissioners a copy of any bull, dispensation, or other instrument which they received from Rome, on penalty of misdemeanor, and expulsion from the kingdom. Most of the English Catholics, and a considerable number of Irish politicians and ecclesiastics were favourable to this settlement, and Monseignor Quarrantotti, who held certain vicarial powers from Pius VII., then a prisoner in France, recommended its acceptance; but the great bulk of the bishops, clergy, and people of Ireland passionately rejected it. They preferred not to obtain Emancipation to accepting it on terms which would destroy the independence of their Church.

The Catholic question lost some of its greatest advocates; Grattan and Curran died, Plunket and Canning were hampered by office, but still it progressed. It was considered a fact of happy import when the Duke of Wellington's brother became Lord Lieutenant, and brought over to Dublin a wife who went openly to Mass to the horror

of all loyal persons. It was counted something when the
services of Catholics to the empire were formally acknowledged. In the contest with Napoleon they had contributed to win battles which are still among the achievements Englishmen are proudest to recall; and in a rare
interval of generosity the Duke of Wellington reminded
the House of Lords that Ireland furnished at least half the
troops with which he had encountered the power of France,
and that it was "mainly to Irish Catholics" England owed
her predominance in Europe in that era.

But it was a quarter of a century after the Union before
the Catholic Association, which finally won Emancipation,
was founded. That body, which grew from slight begin-
nings, gradually drew into its bosom the nobility, the
clergy, who became its devoted agents, the middle class,
and finally the whole Catholic people. Richard Sheil
excited public spirit from the tribune of the Corn Exchange—its ordinary place of meeting—by a passionate
persuasive rhetoric, which afterwards swayed a less sympathetic audience in Westminster, and Wyse, Woulfe and
others were busy in its counsels. But O'Connell was its
life and soul. All the leisure which could be stolen from
a professional life engrossed by profitable business was
given to the Association. Projects which had been tried
and abandoned by the Catholics before, were taken up
anew, and patiently worked out to practical success,

Catholic rent was universally collected by Catholic churchwardens, and local disputes were settled by umpires appointed by the Association. Neither rent, nor churchwardens, organization, nor oratory, were new agencies in Catholic affairs; but they had never been employed so persistently or successfully before.

There was only one class over whom the influence of the Protestant gentry was still supposed to defy competition, the tenants at will. For the ordinary state of a tenant at will made submission to his landlord a necessity, almost a duty. In Ulster the Scotch settlers had obtained, and their descendants had jealously preserved, certain obvious rights, such as the right to enjoy undisturbed possession while they paid a reasonable rent, of the houses they built, and the farms they fenced and improved. But in the descendants of the original owners of the land no such rights were recognised; they held on a tenure the like of which was elsewhere unknown to human law. When they were accepted as tenants on confiscated estates, after the supply of strangers was exhausted, they had often been put into possession of land left as bare as the great desert by civil war; and the houses they built, the fences they erected, and the trees they planted became immediately, under a law made for their special behoof, the property of the landowner. Swift in his semi-ironical way recommended a parson whose church was dilapidated to give it to the

Papists, and when they had repaired it he might take it back. The landlord improved on this hint; he hired naked land to the Papists, and when they had put it in working order took it back at his discretion. Whenever a farm became valuable by the labour of the tenant, it was a common practice to give him the choice to pay an increased rent, or to turn out. The tenant commonly had no resource but to accept the landlord's terms; for the population had nearly doubled since the Union, and the decay of trade and commerce threw the whole people upon agriculture. Extortionate rents were paid or promised (for they were often intentionally fixed at an impossible amount to ensure submission in other respects), and the tenants were in consequence poorer, worse clad, worse fed, and worse housed, than the people of any civilised country in the world.* It was this class so oppressed and degraded who won the final victory. At the general election of 1826 three counties, where the landlords had been supreme since the Revolution, elected candidates sanctioned by the Association. The forty-shilling freeholders, often day labourers, holding patches of land, or a cottage and garden, at best small farmers, whose votes had been

---

* "In various parts of Ireland I know land to be let one hundred per cent. over its fair value. I think, generally, land is let twenty or thirty per cent. above its value."—Evidence of the Right Rev. Dr. Doyle, before a Select Committee of the House of Commons.

exacted as punctually as their rent, voted for emancipators.

In Monaghan they defeated the Blayneys and Shirleys, in Louth the Jocelyns and Fosters, and in Waterford ejected a member of the predominant house of Beresford, which up to that time had held Ireland in its grasp, as the Dundasses held Scotland. These successes encouraged the Association to a bolder step, and two years later they determined to procure the election of a Catholic, who was by law declared incapable of sitting or voting.* The choice naturally fell on O'Connell, whose name would excite the widest enthusiasm. He stood for Clare against a member of the Wellington Government. The gentry to a man, whether for or against Emancipation, fought a desperate battle for their long established authority. The forty-shilling freeholders of nearly every parish in the county, with the priest at the head of his congregation, marched to the hustings and voted for O'Connell. It would have required less courage to have gone into battle, than to defy the agent and the driver armed with ejectments, who stood by taking note of their delinquency.' But a

---

* Patrick Vincent Fitzpatrick, afterwards Secretary of the fund known as the O'Connell Tribute, remembered, that when he was a boy, John Keogh told his father, who was the publisher for the Catholics in that day, that whenever an Irish county elected a Catholic, Emancipation would be achieved. On this hint the attempt was made, and its success amply justified Keogh's prediction

Q

pitched battle could not yield more decisive results than this contest; it was the proximate cause of Emancipation.

The Catholics were at length emancipated in 1829; and now, surely, their enemies suggested, they must be contented and grateful for evermore? Perverse must the people be who, having got what they asked, are not satisfied. Let us see. What they asked was to be admitted to their just share, or, at any rate to some share, of the government of their native country, from which they had been excluded for five generations. But on the passing of the Emancipation Act not a single Catholic was admitted to an office of authority, great or small. The door was opened, indeed, but not a soul was permitted to pass in. There were murmurs of discontent, and the class who still enjoyed all the patronage of the State, the Church, the army, the magistracy, and the public service, demanded if there was any use in attempting to conciliate a people so intractable and unreasonable?* The Catholic Association, which had won the victory, was rewarded for its public spirit by being dissolved by Act of Parliament. Its leader,

---

* More than a generation before, Catholics had been made eligible to serve on juries, but in some counties, during the whole period, a Catholic was never admitted to serve on a trial where the prisoner was a Catholic. They had been declared competent to hold leases, but no leases were forthcoming when they asked for them. In all these cases it was deemed sufficient to admit the principle, and highly ungrateful and unreasonable of the Catholics to ask any more.

who had been elected to the House of Commons, had his election declared void by a phrase imported into the Emancipation Act for this special purpose. The forty-shilling freeholders, whose courage and magnanimity had made the cause irresistible, were immediately deprived of the franchise. By means of a high qualification and an ingeniously complicated system of registry, the electors in twelve counties were reduced from upwards of a hundred thousand to less than ten thousand. Englishmen cannot comprehend our dissatisfaction. Suppose the Anti-Corn-Law League, when it won a victory not more salutary, had been ignominiously suppressed; that Free Trade, though conceded in principle, had been rendered abortive in action; that Manchester and Bradford, Rochdale and Staleybridge, had been disfranchised by Act of Parliament, and Richard Cobden studiously insulted in the statute that established the principles for which he had contended, the result of the victory would scarcely have been universal contentment and gratitude among the manufacturers of England.

But at least the intention and *animus* of this great act of justice ought to be recognised, which English statesmen had the courage to concede without the consent, and probably against the wishes, of the English people? Emancipation could not have been carried through parliament if there were not a body of statesmen there eager to see justice done because it was justice, and outside, a corps of publicists who had prepared the public mind of the middle class to accept it. But the motives of the proposer were widely different. The Duke of Wellington explained himself explicitly to his colleagues, and especially to his royal master. He did not ask him to yield, that right might be done and a long-delayed debt paid, but simply because it was no longer safe to resist. There was now, he declared, a majority in the House of Commons resolved on Emancipation, who would not suppress the Association or disfranchise the forty-shilling freeholders till this measure was passed. He might dissolve this ill-conditioned parliament, and appeal to the still vigorous bigotry of the people of England, but he was confronted with the danger, after O'Connell's success, that the staff of the Corn Exchange would be transferred bodily to the House of Commons. He could not even promote an Irish county member to be a Peer or a Minister, from fear that Sheil or O'Gorman Mahon would be immediately elected in his place. Nor was this the worst. The Irish people might, and probably would, stop the supplies to a church and an aristocracy which insulted and oppressed them; and the House of Commons could not be counted on for putting down even rebellion unless concessions were made. These were the Duke's motives. The insensibility of a people who were not touched by this noble generosity has been naturally a theme of indignant reproof down to our own day.*

The project of a veto on the appointment of Bishops

---

* The Duke wrote to Peel (Sept. 12th, '28) :—"If I could believe that the Irish nobility and gentry would recover their lost influence, the just influence of property, without making those concessions, I would *not* move." To Dean Phillpotts, who urged him to concede nothing, he wrote—"They (Parliament) will not put down the Association, they will not even put down rebellion, if it should occur, unless concessions should be made." To the King he disclosed the imminent danger of delay. "I do not suggest an impossible hypothesis to your majesty, when I state the possibility (I might state it more strongly) of the Roman Catholic tenantry of the country refusing to pay tithes or rents. The clergy and the landlords might have recourse to the law. But how is the law to be enforced? How can they distrain for rent or tithes upon millions of tenants? This measure which will most probably be the first of resistance and rebellion in Ireland, will occasion the ruin of all your majesty's loyal subjects residing in that country, and of many in this; and it must be observed that it will give the rebellion a vast resource of money of which your majesty's loyal subjects will have been deprived.",
—The Duke of Wellington's "Despatches and Correspondence," Vol. II., p. 135.

The Duke's Irish correspondents took a still gloomier view of the situation. The Knight of Kerry, an Irish proprietor and Privy Councillor, warned the Duke that there was grave danger of an insurrection headed by Irishmen from America, whether the leaders desired it or not, and that on this occasion the Catholic gentry could no longer be counted on as allies of England. "Every parish," he said, "is a regiment . . . we hold our lives at the mere discretion of the Catholic population. I never knew the Protestant mind of Ireland dismayed before." He advised immediate concessions, without which this country was lost, or only be retained by means and in a condition worse than its loss.—*Ibid.* Vol. IV., p. 213.

formed no part of the measure. It had long been abandoned before the determined resistance it encountered; but from that time forth the English Government have constantly striven to employ their influence in foreign affairs to the same end. While the Emancipation Act had barely become law, the Duke of Wellington wrote to his kinsman, Lord Burghesh, at that time in the diplomatic service, in relation to a vacancy in the Catholic See of Waterford. The Duke wished an English ecclesiastic, Dr. Weld, subsequently Cardinal Weld, to be appointed to it, and was very emphatic on the point. "I shall be very much obliged (he wrote) if you will lose no time in exerting all your private influence to have this appointment made."*

Emancipation was speedily followed by a Reform of the House of Commons. In England a sweeping and salutary change was made both in the franchise, and in the distribution of seats; but Ireland did not obtain either the number of representatives she was demonstrably entitled to by population and resources, or such a reduction of the franchise as had been conceded to England. The Whigs were in power, and Ireland was well-disposed to the party. The original Whigs who had curbed the inordinate power

---

* Letter of the Duke of Wellington to Lord Burghesh, Oct. 19, 1829. Lord Burghesh afterwards became Earl of Westmoreland.

of the Crown in the Revolution of 1688 were, it is true, the chief authors of the Penal Code; but their successors, a century later, retained the love of political liberty without the canker of religious bigotry. In Parliament, and in a Press which influenced opinion in a decisive manner at the beginning of the nineteenth century, they insisted on justice to Ireland, and in the first place the Emancipation of the Catholics. Their leaders refused to take office from George III., on condition of being silent on this question, and the writings of Sydney Smith, and Jeffrey, contributed to the final victory in as large a degree as the integrity of Grenville and Grey. But the idea of treating Ireland on perfectly equal terms, and giving her the full advantage of the Union which had been forced on her, did not exist in the mind of a single statesman of that epoch.

After Emancipation and Reform, O'Connell had a fierce quarrel with the Whigs, during which he raised the question of Ireland's right to be governed exclusively by her own Parliament. The people responded passionately to his appeal. The party of Protestant Ascendancy had demanded the Repeal of the Union before Emancipation, but that disturbing event altered their policy, and they withheld all aid from O'Connell. After a brief time he abandoned the experiment, to substitute for it an attempt to obtain what was called "justice to Ireland." In furtherance of this project he made a compact with the Whigs that the Irish Party under his lead should support them in parliament. The Whigs in return made fairer appointments to judicial and other public employments, restrained jury packing, and established an unsectarian system of public education; but the national question was thrown back for more than a generation.

In 1840-1 O'Connell revived the question of Repeal, on the ground that the Union had wholly failed to accomplish the end for which it was said to be designed. Instead of bringing Ireland prosperity, it had brought her ruin.

The social condition of the country during the half-century, then drawing to a close was, indeed, without parallel in Europe.

The whole population were dependent on agriculture. There were minerals, but none found in what miners call "paying quantities." There was no manufacture except linen, and the remnant of a woollen trade, slowly dying out before the pitiless competition of Yorkshire. What the island chiefly produced was food; which was exported to richer countries to enable the cultivator to pay an inordinate rent. Foreign travellers saw with amazement an island possessing all the natural conditions of a great commerce, as bare of commerce as if it lay in some byeway of the world where enterprise had not yet penetrated. Harbours looking towards the prosperous Western world were completely vacant; harbours looking towards the East were occupied only by ships which carried raw produce and human food to England. There was no foreign trade; the wines of Spain and Portugal, the silks of France, the drugs and spices of the East, the timber of the North still reached the island through England. The noble quays of the Liffey, which would rival the Lung Arno if Dublin were the seat of a national Government, held only a few coal barges and fruit boats. Similar decay was nearly universal. The provincial towns in general had an unprosperous or bankrupt look. There was scarcely a county which could not show some public work begun before the Union and now a ruin. When an Irish gentleman visited other countries the contrast turned his blood to gall; Lord Cloncurry declared that there was more misery in Dublin than in all Europe besides.

The condition of the two classes who live by agriculture furnished a similar contrast. The great proprietors were two or three hundred—the heirs of the Undertakers, for the most part, and Absentees; the mass of the country was owned by a couple of thousand others, who lived in splendour, and even profusion; and for these the peasant ploughed, sowed, tended, and reaped a harvest which he never shared. Rent, in other countries, means the surplus after the farmer has been liberally paid for his skill and labour; in Ireland it meant the whole produce of the soil except a potato-pit. If a farmer strove for more, his master knew how to bring him to speedy submission. He could carry away his implements of trade by the law of distress, or rob him of his sole pursuit in life by the law of eviction. He could, and habitually did, seize the growing crop, the stools and pots in his miserable cabin, the blanket that sheltered his children, the cow that gave them nourishment. There were just and humane landlords, men who performed the duties which their position imposed, and did not exaggerate its rights; but they were a small minority. The mild Berkeley, in his day, spoke of certain Irish proprietors as "vultures with iron bowels;" and landlords of this type were still plentiful. There was nowhere in Europe a propertied class who did so little for the people, and took so much from them. The productive power of an estate was often doubled and quadrupled by the industry of the farmers; and its rental rose accordingly. In later times rent shot up with war prices, with Protection, with the system of con-acre (under which small patches were let at an exorbitant rate to labourers to grow potatoes), but when any of these stimulants was withdrawn they did not come down. Rents impossible to be paid were kept on the books of an estate, and arrears duly recorded to hold the tenant in perpetual subjection. For, in addition to his labour, the landlord required his vote and sundry menial services. The Lady Bountiful of the parish—for women are more unfeeling and inconsiderate in their exactions than men—often insisted on the children being sent to a proselytizing school, on pain of immediate ejectment. O'Connell sometimes demanded how they would like to have it made compulsory on them to send their children to be educated at Maynooth on pain of forfeiting their estates? but they regarded the absurd comparison with proper contempt. The food of the peasant was potatoes with a little milk or salt; flesh-meat he rarely tasted, except when he went as a harvest labourer to England, "to earn the rent." The country was famous for the production of butter, and the growth of beef and mutton, and especially of pork; but butter, beef, mutton, or pork was nearly as unknown as an article of diet among the peasantry as among the Hindoos. Of this food, such as it was, there was rarely enough. Famines were frequent, and every other year destitution killed a crowd of peasants. For a hundred and fifty years before, whoever has described the condition of Ireland—English official, foreign visitor, or Irish patriot—described a famine more or less acute. Sometimes the tortured serfs rose in nocturnal jacquerie against the system; and then a cry of "rebellion" was raised, and England was assured that these intractable barbarians were again, (as the indictment always charged), "levying war against the King's majesty." There were indeed causes enough for national disaffection, but of these the poor peasant knew nothing; he was contending for so much miserable food as would save his children from starvation. There were sometimes barbarous agrarian murders—murders of agents and bailiffs chiefly, but occasionally of landlords. It would be shameful to forget that these savage crimes were often the result of savage provocation. Agrarian murders were made a constant reproach to the country; but by agrarian murders critics always meant the wild vengeance of the trampled peasantry, never the killing by starvation and exposure (in our own day known as "extermination") which so often provoked their reprisals. Lord Melbourne (when Chief Secretary for Ireland) uttered a judgment on one victim which unhappily might stand for many of his class. "If one-half of what is told me of him be true," he wrote, "and it comes from many different quarters, if he had forty thousand lives there would have been no wonder if they had been all taken."* The peasants often sympathised with these crimes—a fact painful and horrible to contemplate; but let us remember that all England went into a delirium of joy when the knife of Fulton struck down the favourite of Charles I.; for to hate their enemies is the human instinct which religion finds it hardest to control. The agricultural labourer was in a still worse condition than the farmer. Wages in Ireland in the reign

---

* Mr. M'Cullagh Torrens' *Life of Lord Melbourne*, Vol. I., p. 283.

of Queen Victoria were often lower than they had been in
England in the reign of Queen Elizabeth. Tipperary had
the reputation of being an insubordinate county; the Railway Commission Report of the state of the labourers at
this time in Tipperary may perhaps help to explain the
fact. "They go through the fields and gather the wild
weeds, and boil them with salt, and they live on them
without even a potato to eat along with them." They
were not content with their condition; to be content would
have been base and ignominious. It is charged that the
Irish peasant was thriftless and ignorant. He was not free
from the faults slavery and misery engender; how could he
be indeed? It must be admitted that he was not trained
in the minor morals of order and foresight, and, for education, had been merely taught to sign his name and read
his prayer-book. But his faults of character were mainly
the direct result of law. His grandfather was a Papist, to
whom it was a transportable offence to teach the multiplication-table; his father was not permitted to possess landed
property, arms, or the franchise; and in his own day there
were no public schools at which his religion and his
race were not bywords of scorn. The people, denounced
as lazy Celts, were performing tasks which were too
laborious for the natives to endure in England, France,
and the United States; had made settlements in the
Tropics among the half civilised races of South America,

and on the foggy coasts of Newfoundland; and were squabbling with emancipated slaves for the fatal wages of the West Indian planter.

The country was naked of timber, the cabins of the peasantry were squalid and unfurnished. Mr. Carlyle reproves a lazy, thriftless people, who would not perform the simple operation of planting trees; and Mr. Froude frowns upon cottages whose naked walls are never draped by climbing roses or flowering creepers. But how much more eloquent is fact than rhetoric? The Irish landlords made a law that when the tenant planted a tree it became not his own property but his master's; and the established practice of four-fifths of the Irish landlords, when a tenant exhibited such signs of prosperity as a garden, or a white-washed cabin, was to reward his industry by increasing his rent. Peasants will not plant or make improvements on these conditions, nor, I fancy, would philosophers.

In the early part of the present century, when the condition of the peasantry was considerably improved, it is officially recorded that one-half of them lived in mud-wall cabins of one room. The women and many of the men went habitually barefooted and half-clad, under a moist and stormy sky. An eminent French publicist* visiting Ireland in 1824, declared that he had seen the Indian in

---

* De Beaumont.

his wigwam, and the negro in his chains, but that the condition of the Irish tenant at will was worse than that of the savage or the slave. And above them they saw a gay, luxurious, but frank and fearless aristocracy, and a Church which was to them as Dives was to Lazarus. The gentry had grown accustomed to regard the whole produce of the land as their natural right. If this claim was disputed, a shriek of remonstrance was addressed to the Government, and judges in red robes, or soldiers in red coats, made short work of the dissentients. "The country was garrisoned," to employ the language of Michael Sadleir, the political economist, "to protect the property of those whose conduct occasioned all the evils under which Ireland had groaned for centuries . . and which would not be worth a day's purchase were the proprietors its sole protectors."*

It may well seem incredible, if these sufferings existed, that any community could witness them without burning impatience and a passionate desire of resistance; but familiarity with wrong, like familiarity with vice, is fatal to the sentiment of moral indignation. The long endurance of the people has been the subject of two theories among notable English writers, which it is difficult to

---

* English Toryism had even in my eyes about as much to say for itself as any other form of doctrine, but Irish Toryism is the downright proclamation of brutal injustice, and all in the name of God and the Bible ! It is almost enough to make one turn Mahometan,—*John Sterling.*

reconcile. When they resisted they are described as
turbulent Celtic savages whose ferocity vindicated the
rigour of Cromwell, and for whom the sword was the only
practicable ruler. And latterly, the fact that they did not
resist more effectually has been assumed to justify their
tyrants, by proving that they were fit for no better treatment.
In truth they continued to endure these wrongs
because they were deprived of their natural leaders by the
policy which dictated the Penal laws. The moment the
Catholic Association gave them leaders whom they could
trust, their pluck and enthusiasm instantly revived. "It
was not the priests who kindled the people," says the
historian of the Catholic Association, "it was the people
who kindled the priests." And it is necessary to remember
that to resist the smallest reform in Ireland the whole
power of England was always ready to engage itself. The
absentee proprietors, two or three hundred peers and
patricians resident in London, to whom the Administration
of the day was as accessible as the mayor
of a city is to the principal burgesses, ruled Ireland for
their proper interest. Their partisans poisoned English
opinion against Irishmen, generation after generation, by
systematic calumny; and bitter hatred of the Celtic
name, race, language, and character, will be found to taint
English literature from Milton to Thackeray. Time, we
are assured by benevolent critics, will extinguish this

sentiment, which is possible; but as we have been waiting several centuries, the process is perhaps a little dilatory.

The garrison of officials in Dublin, and all who lived on their favours, pursued the same policy. The Castle press obtained large subsidies under the pretence of advertising proclamations relating to local crimes, and, to justify these profitable announcements, the Castle journals made it a point to insist that crime was constantly on the increase. The name of rebellion was affixed on the slightest local disturbance, and rebel was the ordinary designation of a prisoner charged with assault or riot. When Sir Arthur Wellesley was Chief Secretary, he applied himself to this branch of his duties with his usual directness; and elaborate instructions may be found in his correspondence how to feed the subsidised journals with advertisements, so discreetly that the accounts might always be ready to be produced before parliament.* Newspapers were not the only offenders. It was the interest of the gentry to distract attention from the just complaints of their tenantry, and they kept the Castle flooded with reports of disloyal projects and proceedings.

But the system did not rest within these traditional limits. *Espionage* has been recognised as a permissible instrument of Government, base, but necessary; but there

---

* Wellington Despatches.

is a spy system which brings infamy not only on its agents, but on its employers. In the State Trials connected with the United Irishmen, a counsel constantly engaged in the defence of the political prisoners, was a hired agent of the the Government, employed to betray the secrets of his clients. In the civil struggle of the Catholics for their rights, a Protestant journalist conspicuous for his sympathy and alliance with the Catholics, was hired to purloin, and transmit their confidential documents to the Cabinet in London.* Among the peasantry the process of treachery was simpler; the spy or delator commonly stimulated, and often invented, the offences which it was his interest to disclose.

The state of public education was a peculiar scandal. For the Protestant lad of the middle class there were endowed schools, where he got an education almost free, and an opulent University with furnished scholarships, fellowships, church patronage, and other dazzling prizes. For the Catholic lad, unless in the rare instances when he could be sent to the Continent or to the Catholic colleges maintained in England, the State had decreed ignorance and idleness. Up to 1832 the children of the industrious classes were taught in Hedge Schools—schools held in the open air for want of the shelter of a roof. The teaching

---

* See D. F. MacCarthy's Early Days of Shelley.

was probably rude and chaotic, but it used to be believed that the hedge schoolmasters were strong in classics, and it is certain that they sometimes sowed seed which under the care of Irish colleges in France, Spain, and Belgium ripened into famous scholarship and eminent achievements.

The struggling peasant bore the whole burthen of the Established Church. We have seen how, early in the eighteenth century, the landowners, in Parliament assembled, adroitly transferred the burthen to the tenantry. The peasant paid also a moiety of the Poor Rate. But these were equitable provisions compared to the law regulating County Cess. The Grand Jury presentments amounted to more than a million annually, spent, at the discretion of the gentry, on police to protect their property, hospitals to receive their sick dependants (which provided also convenient employments for their favourites), and on roads, sometimes made in shameless disregard of public claims, for their personal convenience. And all this expenditure by an iniquitous law was thrown exclusively upon the tenantry. The wildest inventions of political satire are transcended by the history of local taxation in Ireland.

A long monopoly of power is a feast that not only intoxicates but besots. The Protestants in Ireland had been like Roman citizens in Gaul or British officials in

India. They not merely affected airs of pre-eminence and patronage, but honestly believed themselves a superior race. In Edmund Burke's time many Protestant gentlemen in Ireland, as he tells us, never conversed with a Catholic in their lives, unless to give directions to a workman, or to ask their way across country. A few months before he introduced the Emancipation Bill, the Duke of Wellington threatened to dismiss Mr. Villiers (the Earl of Clarendon known to the last generation) for having invited to dinner the Catholic leader, Richard Shiel, afterwards the darling of London clubs.* So late as 1841, Mr. Thackeray, visiting a Catholic squire who cultivated more land than any gentleman farmer in Leinster, and in another pursuit employed more workmen than any manufacturer in Dublin, learned with amazement that the parson, who lived close to his gate, though they maintained friendly relations, would not break bread with him.† But the assumption of a gentleman was modest, compared to the haughty superiority which a clown or a shop-boy in Ulster, who sang psalms on a Sunday, affected towards his equal, who went to Mass.

Of the Irish Protestants the Presbyterians were a moiety. The liberality which they had shown towards

---

* Greville's "Memoirs."
† "Irish Sketch Book."

Catholics a half-century before, had nearly disappeared. Many of them were Orangemen, and some of their most conspicuous ministers were as vehement Unionists as their predecessors had been vehement United Irishmen. The *regium donum** brought the ecclesiastical spokesmen of their Church into connection with the State, a relation which among the descendants of the Covenanters, as formerly among the Huguenots, gradually replaced vigilant distrust by a lazy acquiescence in the will of the Government. It was the fixed policy of the landlords to keep alive sectarian feelings. The Orangemen still found leaders among them, and were encouraged to commemorate the last battle in which the Catholics were defeated, by musters and processions of armed men, with offensive banners and insulting music. They were taught to fear that the Catholics of Ulster would destroy them if they were not for ever on the alert. The Catholics in that province were then in a minority, and unarmed, but the fears of oppressors are easily excited. Titus Oates persuaded the people of London that a handful of panic-stricken Catholics were about to rise and massacre them. Danton and his agents persuaded the people of Paris that their lives and liberties were in danger from a few royalists shut up in prison; and it is probable that the alarm

---

* A State grant to the Presbyterian Church.

was not wholly simulated. Now and then a rumour was mysteriously spread that the Catholics of the South were about to invade Ulster, and it was not an uncommon event to read of the wrecking of a Catholic village in the North, on some Orange anniversary, by way of retaliation for the invasion which never came off. And many who had no share in the system were supposed to wink complacently at it. There is a peasant song which paints with touches of genuine feeling the agony of the tortured Catholic in the hands of the tormentor :—

> "They came in the mornin' scoffin' and scornin',
> Saying Ware you racked? Ware you sore abused?
> Oh base deluders, you're worse nor Judas
> Who sowld our Saviour to the wicked Jews."

The towns were ruled in a fashion which the Mussulman could scarcely excel. Up to 1842 the bulk of the rates, and generally some exceptional and offensive burthen in addition, were borne by the Catholics; all the offices and employments were enjoyed by favourite lackeys of the minority, appointed by a governing body exclusively Protestant. The charter toast of public institutions was, "To Hell with Pope and Popery, brass money, and wooden shoes."*

---

* "Brass money and wooden shoes." Ever since the Irish Government of James II., when the coin was debased by that prince, a Catholic victory was assumed to involve the issue of brass money in lieu of silver; and among the atrocities attributed to his allies, the French, was the design of forcing *sabots* upon the people. As the majority of them

They had employed their exclusive power, as exclusive power is commonly employed, to plunder the funds entrusted to their management. It was several years after the Corporations of England and Scotland had been reformed, before a reform, as it was called, was accomplished in these institutions. The bulk of them were abolished, confessedly to prevent them falling into the hands of the Catholic majority, and the few which were preserved in the chief towns were granted only limited functions, and fenced with an inordinate property qualification, in shameful contrast to the qualification established in London, Manchester, or Birmingham.

To keep the people divided, not only was creed set against creed, but district against district. Party fights and faction fights were permitted and encouraged. In faction fights one parish, or one family, matched itself against some other, without any relation to opinions. Provincial and local jealousies were common. The Munster Irish disliked the Irish of Ulster, and despised the Irish of Connaught. I remember when a boy, hearing an Ulster peasant, who went harvesting to England, boast that whenever he was reproached with the rags and dirt

---

went barefooted under the existing regime, the prospect was not very alarming; and Swift, when Wood's halfpence were forced upon Ireland, for the profit of a mistress of George I., discovered that base money is not an exclusively Popish invention.

of Connaughtmen, he used to declare that they came from
an island like the Isle of Man, a day's sail from Ireland!
It would be unjust to attribute altogether to the policy of
the gentry or the Castle a practice which had its origin, to
some extent, in the intense individuality of the Celt.

The minority held all their pleasant monopolies on the
condition of satisfying England that they were in the right
and their victims in the wrong. England was not hard to
satisfy on this point, and the Undertakers never failed to
keep a press at work to blacken the people. But at
bottom they were pursuing their own policy, not England's
Irish Whigs insist that had Tories not maintained an
insolent and aggressive pulpit, and a venomous stipendiary
press, a good understanding might have grown up between
the two countries. This privileged minority constituted all the Ireland known to London Society. The
stately courteous gentleman, the head of some historic
house, idealized in Lever's later romances, the vulgar,
boastful spendthrift, speaking a superfine broken English,
and repudiating all sympathy with his native country,
caricatured in Thackeray's novels, as far as they existed at
all, were specimens of the Anglo-Irish. Here and there
one met the amazing phenomenon of an Irish family
who repudiated Ireland. "Your daughter has a charming
Munster accent," an English traveller said to a matron of
quality economising in Hanover. "No, sir," the lady

replied, " you deceive yourself, a Sheffielde of Sheffieldestown never had an Irish accent." These were the Cromwellian gentry for the most part. "Butterflies at London," as an incensed critic has described them, " but gadflies at home." The native gentleman of Milesian descent, painted somewhat *en beau* by John Banim and Lady Morgan in novels now little read, had Paris for his capital rather than London. The Leaders of society in Dublin belonged to neither of these classes. They were invariably great English officials, generally more foreign in spirit and manners than even in blood. They were like telegraph posts, dry, sapless, inflexible, never taking root in the soil, and never putting forth any friendly shade.

To understand the base parody of justice which existed in that era, the reader must consider the position of a Greek or a Slav before a court of Mussulmans. The idea of equality before the law was unknown. A Liberal Lord Lieutenant* excited fierce indignation among a large class of highly respectable persons by refusing to permit the master of an Orange lodge, who had been tried for murder, and who has since been tried for a second murder, to act as sub-sheriff, and select juries throughout a northern county. This man's name was Sam Gray, and his character was so little a matter of doubt, that several years before

---

* The Earl of Mulgrave, afterwards Marquis of Normanby.

he was selected for official distinction, the Chief Secretary in Ireland, Lord Francis Leveson Gower, wrote of him to the Prime Minister, the Duke of Wellington, as "a man who had killed one Catholic, and would be very happy to kill another." And another he actually was tried for killing some years later, and a second time escaped punishment, it was believed, by the connivance of his confederates in the jury box. The judges were selected on a principle not widely different. At this time a brace of legal gladiators, who had become intolerable to the House of Commons by violence and indiscretion, were sent to administer what was called justice in Ireland.* In the safe obscurity of the Petty Sessions Court, where the squires could work their will without control or comment, transactions took place which the most partisan judge would condemn. It was worst in Ulster; there were more than eleven hundred magistrates there, of whom scarce a dozen were Catholics. In many baronies and in several counties, there was not a single Catholic in the commission. Frequently the entire bench and all its servants were members of an Orange lodge. It was often

---

* "He (Peel) had been fortunate in early disembarrassing himself of the Orange counsellors, who conducted his Irish Questions when in opposition; vacant judgeships had opportunely satisfied the recognized and respectable claims of Mr. Serjeant Jackson and Mr. Lefroy."—Mr. Disraeli's *Life of Lord George Bentinck.*

scarcely better in the South. In Tipperary, a peculiarly Catholic shire, there were a hundred and seventy-eight magistrates, of whom a hundred and sixty were Protestants.*

The ecclesiastical Establishment erected by Henry and Elizabeth was still in possession of the endowments which these liberal patrons bestowed upon it, and from the Supreme Court down to the Quarter Sessions there were always a multitude of processes for tithe arrears. The costs which fell on the peasants, it was noted, commonly exceeded the amount originally claimed. Offenders were liable to citation before the Ecclesiastical Courts, and a new Ecclesiastical Court was sometimes improvised, when the parson of one parish carried the dilatory tithe payer before the parson of a neighbouring parish, to do equal and impartial justice between them.† They were more

---

* The state of the magistracy recalls the administration of a Christian province of Turkey. In Antrim there were a hundred Protestant magistrates and one Catholic; but Antrim was better treated than its neighbours. In Tyrone, Fermanagh, and Donegal there was a plentiful supply of Protestant magistrates and not a single Catholic. In these counties the proportion of the two creeds among the population was about equal. In Clare, with but a handful of Protestants, there were a hundred Protestant magistrates and only fourteen Catholics, in Limerick a hundred and one Protestants and only seventeen Catholics, in Wicklow, close to the capital, seventy-three Protestants and only four Catholics, and in the metropolitan county ninety-three Protestant and only nineteen Catholics.

† In 1839, a year or two before the date at which this sketch termi-

merciless creditors than the landed gentry, and even in years of famine, it is said, they made no abatement of their claims.

Accompanying the State Church there had been State Schools, but in two-thirds of the parishes there were now no congregations, no school-houses, and no service. There were rectors enjoying pleasant incomes, and bishops making colossal fortunes. By a return laid before parliament it appeared that eleven bishops in less than fifty years had contrived to bequeath to their families an average of a hundred and sixty thousand pounds a piece. The churches erected before the Reformation had been seized and appropriated to the Establishment, and when more were supposed to be necessary they were bountifully supplied, chiefly at the cost of the Catholic ratepayers. Where diocesan schools existed, the teaching proffered to Catholic children was strictly Protestant teaching, with the unconcealed purpose of proselytism. But in these arrangements a cynic remarked, at least the poor were on an apostolic scale; there were more than a million and a half of the people living mainly on alms.

It was sometimes made a boast in those days that rank, property, station, and professional success dis-

---

nates, tithe was converted by law into a rent-charge, and the scandals accompanying its collection abated. But the text describes the condition of Ireland "during the half century then drawing to a close."

tinguished the minority in Ireland who were imperialists and Protestants. It was not an amazing phenomenon, that those upon whom the law had bestowed a monopoly of rank, property, and station, for a hundred and fifty years, should have still maintained the advantage a dozen years after Emancipation.

It was a subject of scornful reproach that the districts inhabited by Protestants were peaceful and prosperous, while the Catholic districts were often poor and disorderly. There is no doubt of the facts; the contrast certainly existed. But the mystery disappears when one comes to reflect that in Down and Antrim the Squire regarded his tenantry with as much sympathy and confidence as a Squire in Devon or Essex, that their sons were trained to bear arms, and taught, from the pulpit and platform, that they belonged to a superior race, that all the local employments, paid out of the public purse, were distributed among them, that they had certain well understood rights over their holdings on which no landlord could safely trench, and that they met their masters, from time to time, in the friendly equality of an Orange lodge; while in Tipperary, the farmer was a tenant at will who never saw his landlord except when he followed the hounds across his corn, or frowned at him from the bench; whose rent could be raised, or his tenancy terminated at the pleasure of his master; who, on the smallest complaint, was carried before a bench of magistrates, where he had no expectation, and little chance, of justice ; and who wanted the essential stimulus to thrift and industry, the secure enjoyment of his earnings.

As a set-off to this long catalogue of discouragements, there were two facts of happy augury. In 1842 half a million of children were receiving education in the National Schools under a system designed to establish religious equality, and administered by Catholic and Protestant commissioners.* And the Teetotal movement was at its height. Thousands were accepting every week a pledge of total abstinence from Father Mathew, a young priest whom the gifts of nature and the accidents of fortune combined to qualify for the mission of a Reformer Born in Tipperary, educated in Kilkenny, and long stationed as a friar in Cork, he knew the people of the South intimately. A sweet and patient disposition, a homely eloquence, impressive mainly from the depth of conviction from which it sprang, a certain air of superiority wholly free from arrogance, though attributable perhaps to his birth in the middle class, and a reputation for practical benevolence, enabled him not only to win the

---

*The National system came into operation in 1831-2. The Established Church offered it a stubborn resistance, because the reading of the Bible was not made compulsory. It was opposed by some of the Catholic clergy, and many of the Presbyterian clergy on other grounds.

hearts but to impress the imagination of the people. They came to speak of him fondly as the Apostle of Temperance. From Munster he made his way to the other provinces, and at this time there was probably no county, and no considerable town, without a Teetotal Society. Public-houses had been shut up, breweries and distilleries thrown out of employment; the quantity of whisky consumed in Ireland had diminished one-half, and crime had diminished in even greater proportion. The enrolled Teetotallers were computed to exceed two millions. His mission had succeeded, in the language of Maria Edgeworth, " beyond all the predictions of experience, all examples from the past and all analogy."

There was the beginning of political reforms also. The Whigs sent a Lord Lieutenant and Chief Secretary to Ireland who for the first time since the fall of Limerick treated the bulk of the nation as the social and political equals of the minority. The minority had been so long accustomed to make and administer the laws, and to occupy the places of authority and distinction, that they regarded the change as a revolt; and Lord Mulgrave and Thomas Drummond as the successors of Tyrconnel and Nugent.

In the interval, since Emancipation, a few Catholics were elected to Parliament, two Catholic lawyers were raised to the bench, and smaller appointments distributed among laymen; each appointment being followed by a groan from the Tory press, as if the Emancipation Act were an instrument intended only for show. A more important change had taken place in the administration of justice under Lord Mulgrave, advised by Thomas Drummond. The exclusion of Catholics from juries was restrained, and the practice of appointing partisans of too shameful antecedents, to public functions was interrupted. Drummond, in official correspondence with a great landowner, reminded him of the forgotten principle that " property had its duties as well as its rights," and the sentiment was received by the gentry with a clamour of horror and execration. They were prepared to deny in terms, as they had long denied in practice, that property had any special duties. But such a truth once published with authority, could no more be extinguished or effaced than a new planet. None of these reforms, moral or political, were more than half a dozen years in operation at this time; none of them except Teetotalism had penetrated the mass of the people; the system they disturbed had lasted more than four generations and moulded the habits and character of the nation.*

---

* It is proper to note that a theory of Irish history has been insisted upon with great vehemence in latter times, that the Irish, so far from being ill used, have been spoiled by too much indulgence. There was probably a similar theory respecting West Indian slavery, and it was doubtless considered very sound among the planters of Jamaica and Barbadoes.

Among the middle class Catholics a great change had taken place. A generation had reached manhood who knew the Penal Laws only by tradition. Their fathers had grown rich in trade or the professions, had purchased land, and shared the excitement of a great political contest, and the sons educated for the most part in English or foreign colleges, or in the Dublin University, laughed at the pretensions of Protestant ascendancy. This was the class destined to form the bulk of the party afterwards known as Young Ireland. But the mass of the people were still poor, uneducated, and hampered by laws of shameful unfairness. The Penal Code had left nearly four millions of them unable to read or write, and nearly a million and a half more who could read but not write.*

The island no longer possessed national trade, manufactures, or local industries; they had all once existed and been destroyed by the jealousy of the stronger nation; the facilities which nature bestowed on it for a foreign commerce, were rendered nugatory by the same influence. The produce of the soil, which alone remained to furnish the population with the necessaries of civilized life, was

---

* The exact figures from the Parliamentary returns are 829,000 females, and 580,000 males above five years, who can only read but not write; 2,142,000 females, 1,623,000 males, who can neither read nor write.

The cause of this ignorance might seem evident after the events narrated above; but we are assured on the best English authority, that it was all owing to the "villanous priests"—who objected to education.

S

squandered in a prodigious and wasting subsidy. It was estimated that half a million sterling was remitted to England monthly, in rent. But there was a political economy as well as a political morality for the special use of Ireland, and accommodating writers were ready to demonstrate that it was of no importance to a country whether its earnings were spent at home or abroad.

This was the condition of Ireland when the Union had had a trial of over forty years. The island which, before the coming of the Dane or the Norman, its own people had made the seat of industrial arts and the School of the West, was now the most ignorant and impoverished of Christian States. The island to which, in latter times, its national Parliament had brought back trade, commerce and prosperity, was sickening under a burthen of paupers without hope of employment, because trade and commerce had disappeared. Is it surprising that the result of the experiment led many men to the conclusion that the connection between Ireland and the dominant country must be put on another footing, or must be brought to an end? On less provocation the sober colonists of North America broke away from the empire, and the grave Belgian *bourgeoisie* broke away from their legislative Union. On less provocation indeed the phlegmatic Hollanders opened their dykes and let in the sea.

It was under these circumstances that O'Connell, for

the second time summoned the Irish people to demand a Repeal of the Union; a just and necessary measure—but one which required, as a condition precedent to success, that a population separated by the wrongs I have passed in review, and by the hereditary prejudices and misconceptions to which they gave birth, should unite as one people, for a common end in which they had a common interest.

APPENDIX.

No. I.—LEARNING AND MISSIONARY LABOURS OF THE ANCIENT IRISH CHURCH.

"Of all the countries of the west, Ireland was, for a long time, that in which alone learning was supported, and throve amid the general overthrow of Europe."—*Guizot's History of France.*

"A school was formed at Armagh, which soon became very famous. Many Irish went from thence, to convert and teach other nations. Many Saxons out of England resorted thither for instruction, and brought from thence the use of letters, to their ignorant countrymen."—*Lord Lyttleton's Life of Henry II.*

"That the Irish were lovers of learning, and distinguished themselves in those times of ignorance, beyond all other European nations, travelling through the most distant lands with a view to improve and communicate their knowledge, is a fact with which I have been long acquainted: as we see them in the most authentic records of antiquity, discharging, with the highest reputation and applause, the functions of Doctors, in France, Germany, and Italy."—*Mosheim's Ecclesiastical History.*

"The Irish nation possesses genuine history several centuries more ancient than any other European nation possesses, in its present spoken language."—*Sir James Mackintosh.*

"Dr. Leland begins his history too late; the ages which deserve an exact inquiry are those times, for such there were, when Ireland was the school of the west, the quiet habitation of sanctity and literature. If you could give a history, though imperfect, of the Irish nation, from its conversion to Christianity to the invasion from England, you would amplify knowledge with new views and new objects."—*Dr. Johnson* (*Boswell's Johnson.*)

No. II.—NO QUARTER TO THE IRISH UNDER THE PARLIAMENT.

"In the year 1641-2, many thousands of the poor innocent people of the county of Dublin, shunning the fury of the English soldiers, fled into thickets and furze, which the soldiers did usually fire, killing as many as endeavoured to escape, or forced them back again to be burned, and the rest of the inhabitants for the most part died of famine."—*Appendix of Clarendon's Hist. of the Irish Reb.*

"The Earl of Warwick, and the officers under him at sea, had, as often as he met with any Irish frigates, or such freebooters as sailed under their commission, taken all the seamen who became prisoners to them of that nation (Ireland), and bound them back to back, and thrown them overboard into the sea, without distinction of their condition, if they were Irish. In this cruel manner very many poor men perished daily; of which the King said nothing, because . . . his Majesty could not complain of it without being concerned in the behalf and in favour of the rebels of Ireland."—*Clarendon.*

"The Marquis of Ormond, in May 1644, had sent Captain Anthony Willoughby with 150 men, which had formerly served in the fort of Galway, from thence to Bristol. The ship which carried them was taken by Swanley, who was so inhuman as throw seventy of the soldiers overboard, under the pretence that they were Irish; though they had faithfully served his Majesty against the rebels during all the time of the war."—*Carte's Ormond.*

No. III.—CROMWELL'S ACCOUNT OF THE PLANTATION.

Protocols and proclamations are not models of veracity; but Cromwell published a "Declaration for the undeceiving of deluded people," which it would be difficult to parallel in history. We know how the Plantators got their lands from the Crown, how the natives were driven out without compensation, to live—if they could live—in the mountains and bogs; how they were treated as public enemies, and the Parliament of England was threatening to extirpate them, when they rose to assert their natural rights to possess their own country, as the Scotch, stimulated by the party to which Cromwell belonged, had already risen. But this is the account of the transaction the Lord Protector issued for the information of mankind: "Englishmen had good inheritances, which many of them purchased with their money; they and their ancestors, from you and your ancestors. They had good Leases from Irishmen, for long times to come; great stocks thereupon, houses and plantations erected at their own cost and charge. They lived peaceably and honestly amongst you. You had generally equal benefit of the protection of England with them; and equal justice from the Laws—saving what was necessary for the State, out of reasons of State, to put upon some few people, apt to rebel upon the instigation of such as you. You broke this union. You, unprovoked, put the English to the most unheard-of and most barbarous Massacre (without respect of sex or age) that ever the Sun beheld. And at a time when Ireland was in perfect Peace."

It is probable that Cromwell was in part misled by his Council in Dublin, who had their own motives for deceiving him; but certain it is that a more utterly untrue and untrustworthy account of a human-transaction has rarely been printed than this declaration of the divine appointed ruler.

No. IV.—RABBLING IN SCOTLAND.

"On Christmas Day, therefore, the Covenanters held armed musters by concert in many parts of the western shires. Each band marched to the nearest manse, and sacked the cellar and larder of the minister, which at that season were probably better stocked than usual. The priest of Baal was reviled and insulted, sometimes beaten, sometimes ducked. His furniture was thrown out of the windows; his wife and children turned out of doors in the snow. He was then carried to the market place, and exposed during some time as a malefactor. His gown was torn to shreds over his head: if he had a prayer book in his pocket it was burned; and he was dismissed with a charge, never, as he valued his life, to officiate in the parish again. The work of reformation having been thus completed, the reformers locked up the church and departed with the keys. . . The disorder spread fast. In Ayrshire, Clydesdale, Nithisdale, Annandale, every parish was visited by these turbulent zealots. About two hundred curates—so the episcopal parish priests were called—were expelled."—*Macaulay's History of England*, Vol. 2, chap. 13.

No. V.—EXTRAIT DU RAPPORT SUR LES TROUPES IRLANDAISES AU SERVICE DE LA FRANCE.

Addressé par le General Arthur Dillon, Deputé à L'Assemblée Nationale.

GUERRE D'AMÉRIQUE, 1779.

Les Troupes Irlandaises ont toujours reclamé de marcher les premiers contre les Anglais. C'est d'après ce principe que le regiment de Dillon demanda et obtint de passer en Amerique au commencement de 1779. Il y fut suivi bientôt après par les deux autres regiments Irlandais, et les details suivants feront connaitre qu'ils ont été de quelque utilité dans cette guerre.

Le premier bataillon du regiment de Dillon que l'on porta a 1000 hommes et par la suite a 1400 s'embarqua à Brest le 5 Avril, 1779, dans l'escadre de M. Lamothe Piquet. A son arrivé à la Martinique M. le Comte d'Estaing qui jusqu'à l'arrivée du renfort avait été trop inferieur en nombre aux Anglais pour rien entreprendre resolut alors d'agir offensivement contre eux.

Il fit embarquer le regiment de Dillon sur son escadre et effectua une descente dans l'île de la Grenade, le 1er. Juillet. Les Anglais ont été obligés de rendre Grenade à discrétion.

La moitié du Bataillon de Dillon se trouva au combat naval du 6 Juillet, où les français remportèrent la victoire.

Le regiment Dillon ayant laissé des detachements à la Grenade fit le reste de la campagne sur l'escadre et debarqua devant Savanah en Georgie au mois de Septembre.

La mauvais temps empecha les communications de l'armée debarquée avec les vaisseaux; on ne peut rassembler assez de troupes pour enlever la place de vive force ce qui donna le temps a 800 ecossais du 71 Reg. anglais de s'y jeter. M. le Comte d'Estaing après plusieurs jours de tranchée ouverte, fit, à la tête des troupes une attaque infructueuse dans laquelle le Major Browne du Regiment Dillon fut tué.

1780.—Au commencement de 1780 le second bataillon du Regiment Walsh s'embarqua pour la Martinique.

La même année une partie du Regiment Dillon se trouva aux trois combats navals livreés dans les Antilles par M. Guichen à l'amiral Rodney. Le bataillon Walsh s'y trouva également.

1781.—700 hommes du régiment de Dillon se trouvèrent au combat naval que le Comte de Grasse livra à l'amiral Hood devant la Martinique le 29 Avril. Ils descendèrent ensuite dans l'île de Tabago. Le regiment Walsh y avait debarqué quelques jours avant. Ces deux corps contribuèrent à la prise de cette île le 21 Juin sous les ordres du General de Bouillé. Ce général voulant profiter de l'absence de l'Escadre anglaise s'embarqua le 15 Novembre avec un corps de 1200 hommes pris dans les regiments Dillon, Walsh et dans d'autres et parut devant l'île St. Eustache la nuit du 25 au 26. Les mesures avaient été parfaitement bien prises ; mais le courant n'ayant pu permettre aux frégates d'approcher de la côte il ne put débarquer que 377 hommes et demeura sans espoir de pouvoir se rembarquer ni d'être joint par le reste des troupes sans être découvert par l'ennemi. Dans cette circonstance difficile, le sang froid et la resolution du General qu'il sut communiquer aux troupes suppléèrent au nombre. Il marcha aux ennemis. Les Irlandais étaient à la tête de la colonne. La surprise fut complète. 840 hommes des troupes Anglaises réglées mirent bas les armes et furent faits prisonniers par moins de la moitié de leur nombre.

1782.—Au commencement de cette année le régiment de Dillon fu employé dans l'armée qui fit le siège de le forteresse de Bremstown Hill dans l'île St. Christophe.

Le Marquis de Bouillé se rendit maître de cette place, après trente et un jours de tranchée ouverte, le 12 Février.

L'île resta aux Français jusqu'à la paix. Le Comte Dillon a été fait gouverneur, le régiment y resta, en grand partie, en garnison, et un détachement de 600 hommes en fut envoyé à St. Domingo.

Vers la fin de l'année le second bataillon du régiment Berwick arriva à la Martinique.

La paix qui fut declarée quelques temps après fit suspendre toute expédition. Ce régiment avait été employé en 1779, sur l'escadre de M. d'Orvilliers. Les mouvements politiques qui ont eu lieu il y a deux ans faisant peut-être craindre une rupture avec les Anglais le ministre se fixa sur le régiment de Walsh à peine revenu d'Amérique pour l'envoyer dans l'Inde où il est en ce moment.

NOTICES OF THE "BIRD'S-EYE VIEW,"

On its original appearance as a Chapter of "Young Ireland."

From THE SPECTATOR.

"We need not say that we cannot always agree in the drift of Sir Charles Gavan Duffy's political criticism. It is a very powerful, and for the most part a very just, indictment against the Irish policy of Great Britain. The brief review of Irish history is one of the most vigorous and one of the most painful 'acts of accusation' against this country which was ever penned, and for English readers one of the most wholesome lessons."

From THE CONTEMPORARY REVIEW.

"Sir Charles Duffy's chapter, entitled 'A Bird's-Eye View of Irish History,' casts a flood of light on the wretched state of affairs in Ireland. Those cruel wrongs belong, 'tis true, to the past; but their effects remain, and our generation is undergoing retribution for the unexpiated crimes of other days."

From THE LIVERPOOL ALBION.

"It is written with a dignity, an eloquence, and above all a tolerance of England and Englishmen, which are sadly wanting in the majority of Irish utterances at the present time. And it presents, with admirable perspicacity, a view of Irish History, and Irish aspirations, with which Englishmen are not familiar, but which they may study with advantage to their own country and to Ireland."

From VANITY FAIR.

"There is furthermore a splendid condensation of Irish History which one can admire as an example of telling journalism, and there are numberless sly references to the events of this present period."

From THE IRISH TIMES.

"Sir Charles Gavan Duffy's Bird's-Eye View of Irish History is a chapter which on account of its style alone could ill be spared from this volume. It is written with great pureness and force."

NOTICES OF THE "BIRD'S-EYE VIEW."

From THE BELFAST NORTHERN WHIG.

"There is no class of Irishmen who will not find much to interest them in the fascinating description and judicious criticisms of this book. The author is dealing with the dead, and deals tenderly with their memory. . . . He has given us a fragment of Irish history characterized by great literary power, which can be read with profit by men of all political views and breathing the purest spirit of patriotism. A marvellously interesting, and almost sensational story."

From THE CORK EXAMINER.

"It is amusing to find so consummate a literary craftsman as Gavan Duffy interrupting his account of the proceedings at Burgh-quay by a History of Ireland from the invasion of the Milesius to the establishment of the *Nation*. But like the great builders of old time, he boldly sacrifices artistic symmetry to practical utility. Practically, this is, perhaps, the most valuable chapter in the book. It is no mere book-maker's summary, but the ripe produce of a life of thought and study. That he exercised a sound discretion in thus sacrificing artistic form to practical utility is proved by the attention which this very chapter has received from the English press. 'If an Englishman,' writes the *Spectator*, 'wishes to know what political shame means, let him read the brilliant chapter of historical review in Sir Charles Gavan Duffy's book on 'Young Ireland,' and *he will feel it for a time a burden almost too great to endure.*"

From THE YORK HERALD.

"In its portraits of living men of the period the volume is indeed valuable and vivid, and most readers will be thankful for the Bird's-Eye View of Irish History which gives them in seventy pages the heads of all they will care to know. Historically and politically the Fragment is of intense interest, and it has already earned a popularity which testifies to the judgment of the reading world, and to the skill with which Sir Gavan Duffy has introduced us to his friends and associates and the times in which they lived and laboured."

From THE BRADFORD OBSERVER.

"It is impossible for a writer to be more studiously fair, more temperate in tone, more desirous to be just to friends and foes alike, than Sir Charles Duffy. . . . One chapter entitled 'A Bird's-Eye View of Irish History,' might be reprinted as a pamphlet with advantage, and scattered broadcast over England."

NOTICES OF EARLIER EDITIONS.

From the *Spectator* (London).

"We need not say that we cannot always agree in the drift of Sir Charles Gavan Duffy's political criticism. It is a very powerful, and for the most part a very just indictment against the Irish policy of Great Britain. The brief review of Irish history is one of the most vigorous and one of the most painful 'acts of accusation' against this country which was ever penned, and for English readers one of the most wholesome lessons."

From the *Freeman's Journal* (Dublin).

"We read it through twice in the large edition, and we are reading it through now in its separate form, and it seems to us on the third reading what it seemed on the first. We regard it as the most fascinating chapter in a very fascinating book, as a masterpiece of luminous condensation, and as a gem of historic writing."

From *United Ireland* (Dublin).

"Whosoever wants to know the main facts and the *rationale* of Irish History will find them enshrined in limpid and flowing English, and will rise from perusing the little book refreshed and proud—not, as often happens, after toiling through Irish histories, weary and dejected."

From the *American* (Philadelphia).

"The historical chapter in Sir Charles Gavan Duffy's 'Young Ireland' was recognised generally as the only readable account of Irish history which had appeared in the English language. It is the story of Ireland's wrongs, told by a decided, but not an extreme Irish patriot, and goes a great way to explain the utter discontent with which the Irish people regard English rule."

From the *Age* (Melbourne).

"As a plea for Irish Home Rule, nothing more brilliant than the chapter entitled 'A Bird's-Eye View of Irish history,' has ever been printed."

THIRD EDITION.
YOUNG IRELAND:
A Fragment of Irish History.

From THE TIMES.

"The gifted and ill-fated Party of Young Ireland certainly deserved an *Apologia*, and it is past dispute that no one could be more competent for the task than Sir Charles Gavan Duffy. Notwithstanding the genuine modesty with which he always attributes the origin of the school (for, in the true sense, it was a school rather than a party) to Thomas Osborne Davis, he will, we think, be always regarded as its true founder . . . The literary quality of the book is remarkable; the style is vivid and graphic."

From THE SATURDAY REVIEW.

"Sir Charles Duffy has many qualifications for his task. With great ability and much literary experience he combines an earnest belief in the justice of his cause; and it may be added that he always writes in the language and the spirit of a gentleman."

From THE SPECTATOR.

"Sir Charles Gavan Duffy's book, large as it is, will have for politicians more than the interest of a novel, as well as more than the instructiveness of a history. It is a book full of life and brilliance, and though it covers only a period of five years, and five years which elapsed between thirty and forty years ago—namely, from 1840-1845,—yet those five years were so full of significant likeness, as well as still more significant unlikeness, to the epoch of the moment, and we are reaping so evidently to-day the evil fruits of the errors committed then, that the record of those five years is full of the most absorbing interest."

From THE EDINBURGH REVIEW.

"These, it seems, were the founders, heroes, and martyrs of the *Nation*, and we are free to confess that the Young Ireland of those days had incomparably more patriotism, eloquence, and energy than their degenerate successors. But even Ireland cannot produce an inexhaustible supply of Davises and Duffys. It is in the nature of all human things— 'In pejus ruere et retro sublapsa referri.'"

From THE DUBLIN REVIEW.

"The remarkable and romantic career of the author serves to stimulate the curiosity of the public; but, independently of these advantages, this book contains literary merit of too high an order, and historical matter of too great value, to allow of its being, under any circumstances, ignored or forgotten."

NOTICES OF "YOUNG IRELAND."

From THE WESTMINSTER REVIEW.

"With all the vividness of historical romance, he places before us the wrongs Ireland has had to endure, the evils inflicted upon her system of land tenure, the restrictions which have crippled her industry, and the efforts made by the Irish patriotic party to redress their grievances. The volume is full of special pleading, but the author's style is so graphic and flowing, his irony so keen and humorous, the manner in which he marshals his statements so terse and lucid, that he has succeeded in rendering his work one of the most popular of the season."

From THE FREEMAN'S JOURNAL.

Apologia pro Sociis Meis: So Sir Gavan Duffy might have fitly named this book. Suppressing himself so far as was at all possible in narrating a history of which he was so great a part, he has devoted unwearied labour and a literary power which has few rivals to the task of raising an enduring memorial to his old associates, friends, and fellow-workmen; and he has done this with an enthusiasm and freshness of zealous conviction which fill every reader of his work with wonder."

From THE IRISHMAN.

"Time after time the author returns to describe, or recall his friends, and every time with a new tenderness and renewed affection—an affection in which we surely can share, who are the heirs of the fruits of their heart's toil. So OSSIAN recalled the companions of his glorious days, the knightly DIARMUID, and OSCAR 'of the gold-deeds.'"

From THE BELFAST NORTHERN WHIG.

"There is no class of Irishmen who will not find much to interest them in the fascinating description and judicious criticisms of this book. The author is dealing with the dead, and deals tenderly with their memory."

From THE CORK EXAMINER.

"This is by far the most valuable contribution to Irish history that we have had for a generation. It tells the story of a memorable epoch with the thorough knowledge of a man who bore in that epoch a great part, with the fairness of a generous nature dealing with friends and foes whose bones are dust, and with the grace, the brilliancy, and the lucid order of a master of literary style."

From THE TABLET.

"The publication of Sir Gavan Duffy's great work, and at such a crisis, is an event surpassing any mere literary incident, however important, and must be regarded as a highly opportune contribution to the understanding, if not the settlement, of the leading political and social Irish questions, which for ages have baffled British statesmen, and appear utterly incomprehensible to the average English mind."

By the same Author.

BALLAD POETRY OF IRELAND.

FORTY-FIRST EDITION.

From the *Dublin Review*, 1846.

"Our readers will hardly require, on our part, any profession of the unaffected satisfaction with which we welcome this delightful volume, and the "Library of Ireland," to which it belongs. It is a great step towards the realisation of that fond dream of a National Literature, which we have long cherished, and which vague and desponding for a while, the events of the last few years have hurried through the successive stages of hopelessness, possibility, feasibleness, and (may we not now say) certainty—with a rapidity which ten years since, the most sanguine would hardly have ventured to anticipate. We would fain believe that Mr. Duffy's eloquent and earnest Introduction represents the feelings of a large section of the educated public in Ireland ; and if this be so, there shall not be wanting a will or a way towards complete success. It would be difficult to speak too highly of this Introduction—equally difficult, we trust, to over-estimate its influence. Without reading one word of the volume, every educated man will at once pronounce that a collection made by such an editor must possess merit of the very highest order. We regard it, indeed, as perfect in its kind—correct, yet calm, passionate, but subdued—and combining enthusiasm and order with that tolerance which makes enthusiasm amicable, and that practical sense which prevents ardour from evaporating in noisy and ineffective display."

From the *Irish Monthly*, 1882.

His (Fr. Meehan's) history of "The Confederation of Kilkenny," was one of the last volumes of that "Library of Ireland," which was really inaugurated by the famous "Ballad Poetry," though M'Nevin's "Irish Volunteers," was nominally volume the first.

From *Davis's Essays.*

"Never was there a book better fitted to advance that perfect nationality to which Ireland begins to aspire."

www.ingramcontent.com/pod-product-compliance
Lightning Source LLC
Chambersburg PA
CBHW031328230426
43670CB00006B/278